THE
FAITH
OF
LEAP

"All the books of Hirsch and Frost are books that need to be written. Very thoughtful and chock-full of insight and practical advice, this brilliant book reminds us that we can—in fact, we must—substitute another narrative for the security-obsessed one that normally drives us if we wish to truly live!"

—**Reggie McNeal**, missional leadership specialist, Leadership
Network; author of *The Present Future* and *Missional Renaissance*

"Imagine the apostle Paul arriving in the metropolis of Ephesus with the sole task of gospeling that city. Now imagine yourself at the edge of your community with the task of gospeling your community. You've got two pockets. Stick in one of your pockets your Bible and in the other *The Faith of Leap*. You're ready. Now go."

—**Scot McKnight**, Karl A. Olsson Professor in Religious Studies,
North Park University; author, *One.Life: Jesus Calls, We Follow*

"There is too much shallow talk these days about the church 'at the margins,' liminality, or 'living on the edge.' Instead, we need people who will teach us how to become capable of such a thing! *The Faith of Leap* does just that. Hirsch and Frost use their manifold gifts to show us why and how adventure, risk, and courage is at the very heart of living life together in God's Mission."

—**David Fitch**, author, *The End of Evangelicalism? Discerning a
New Faithfulness for Mission*; B. R. Lindner Chair of
Evangelical Theology, Northern Seminary

"As Alan and Mike have helped forge and form missional strategy for the church of the twenty-first century, they have now put rubber to the road by exposing nebulously boring faith and pushing toward the trilogy of adventure, courage, and transformation. Read it if you have the guts."

—**Hugh Halter**, author of *The Tangible Kingdom,
TK Primer, AND*, and *Sacrilege*

"I have read everything Hirsch and Frost ever wrote individually or together, and each time their writing kindles my intellectual and missional imagination. *The Faith of Leap* was a wholly different experience. I began reading it with the thought that the church could certainly use a theology of adventure, but within just a few pages, my own heart was ravenous—urged by the call of the wild to which Jesus invites every woman and every man."

—**Linda Bergquist**, church-starting strategist; co-author, *Church Turned Inside Out: A Guide for Designers, Refiners, and ReAligners*

"Christianity has waited its entire history for someone to risk a theology of risk. Who would have thought that its appearance would come in the form of a fireworks festival. . . . A remarkable tour de force."

—**Leonard Sweet**, bestselling author; professor, Drew University and George Fox University

"I am frequently asked what it will take to see church multiplication movements occur in the West. This book hits on one of the most crucial elements we need to release church multiplication movements—if not the most significant missing ingredient. This is, in my opinion, Hirsch and Frost's best work to date and is must reading for anyone who wants to release missional movements."

—**Neil Cole**, author of *Ordinary Hero*, *Church 3.0*, *Journeys to Significance*, and *Organic Leadership*

Shapevine Missional Series

THE FAITH OF LEAP

EMBRACING A THEOLOGY *of* RISK, ADVENTURE & COURAGE

MICHAEL FROST & ALAN HIRSCH

BakerBooks
a division of Baker Publishing Group
Grand Rapids, Michigan

Published by Baker Books
a division of Baker Publishing Group
P.O. Box 6287, Grand Rapids, MI 49516-6287
www.bakerbooks.com

Printed in the United States of America

Library of Congress Cataloging-in-Publication Data
Frost, Michael, 1961–
    The faith of leap : embracing a theology of risk, adventure & courage / Michael Frost and Alan Hirsch.
        p.   cm. — (Shapevine missional series)
    Includes bibliographical references (p.   ) and index.
    ISBN 978-0-8010-1415-4 (pbk. : alk. paper)
    1. Mission of the church. 2. Risk-taking (Psychology)—Religious aspects—Christianity. I. Hirsch, Alan, 1954– II. Title.
    BV601.8.F758 2011
    262′.7—dc22   2011000499

11 12 13 14 15 16 17   7 6 5 4 3 2 1

To the courageous Ross Clifford, for all the risks he's
taken over the years to foster my thinking and writing.

– Michael

To Kim, Maria, and the Hammond family, who threw caution to
the wind to join us in our American adventure.
And to all those Forge pioneers who continue to birth and
nurture the missional church wherever they find it.

– Alan

To Shirley Decker-Lucke, who took a brave step in publishing two out-of-towners like us, and for Chad Allen
and the whole Baker crew for continuing to do so.

To Jon Strother for suggesting the provoca-
tive title, *The Faith of Leap*.
Good one, Jon.

Contents

About the Shapevine Missional Series

The key purpose of Shapevine the organization is to bring the various elements of missional Christianity—namely, church planting movements, urban mission, the emerging church, the missional church movement, the organic/simple church, and marketplace ministries—into meaningful dialogue around the truly big ideas of our time. Consistent with this purpose, the Shapevine Missional Series in partnership with Baker Books seeks to bring innovative thinking to the missional issues of church planting, mission, evangelism, social justice, and anything in between.

We seek to publish both established authors as well as others who have significant things to contribute but have operated largely under the radar.

The series will focus on three distinctive areas:

- **Living—Practical Missional Orthopraxy**
  Orthopraxy is what makes orthodoxy worth having. We yearn for the experience and continual flow of living out the gospel message in our day-to-day lives for the sake of others. The stories and ideas in the Shapevine Missional Series are aimed at providing practical handles and means to wrap our readers' minds around the idea of living as the people of God, sent into the world with the Spirit and impulse of Jesus himself.

- **Learning—Solid Missional Orthodoxy**

  Jesus both lived and proclaimed a theology of a missional God. His was and is a message of mercy, justice, and goodness toward others. It was this message that erupted into the greatest movement in the history of humankind. The same God who sent his only Son now sends those who follow his Son, in the same manner and with the same message. This is at the heart of a missional theology.

- **Leading—Tools for Missional Leadership**

  Our aim is for the books in this series to serve as tools for pastors, organizational leaders, and church members throughout the world to equip themselves and others as they travel the path of faithfulness in the missional life.

As a global interactive forum, Shapevine allows anyone to both learn and contribute at whatever level suits. To learn more, go to www.shapevine.com or contact us at info@shapevine.com.

Alan Hirsch and Lance Ford

Series Editor's Preface

Clearly coming into deeper knowledge and experience of God is a profound adventure into the infinite unknown. Given that we will always be finite creatures, and God always infinite, this adventure is one that is unlikely to ever end. So we might as well get used to the idea of journey, pilgrimage, risk, and exploration.

While we have libraries filled with books about spirituality, and literally tens of millions of books exploring aspects of theology, we have not been able to identify *one* significant book studying the nature of adventure itself—its role in shaping our thinking about God, our experience of life, or our participation in mission, church, or discipleship. Not one! Similarly, there is painfully little exploration on the associated subject of risk, liminality, *communitas*, and its implications in the life of faith and in leadership.

As one of the authors of this book, I found this deficiency shocking, and given that our experience of God and gospel partakes directly of the nature of adventure, and (as we shall see) the Bible has much to say about it, I believe this ought to disturb you, the reader. What insight does this give into how we experience God and existence itself? Is our understanding of these matters now so passive and tedious that we simply miss this most illustrious metaphor of life—one that is so celebrated in myth, narrative, film, and poetry? And what then does this say about the church itself and how we view faith?

We think that nothing less than the renewal and vigor of Christianity, and with it the mission of the church, is bound up with this subject. Within these pages, the reader will find not only a fresh perspective on somewhat tired subjects but also an invigorated sense of *elan vital* along with (hopefully) an increasing desire to partake of a little adventure of one's own.

Together with the other books that are now part of the series, we feel the book you're holding genuinely adds new knowledge to the church and some fresh impetus to partake more vigorously and faithfully in the redemptive mission of God in our day.

> *You proclaim your truth in every age by many voices:*
> *Direct those, we pray, who speak where many listen or write*
> *   where many read;*
> *that they may do their part*
> *in making the heart of your people wise,*
> *its mind sound, and its will righteous!*
> *Amen*

Alan Hirsch
Shapevine series editor

The End of the Beginning

Introduction

A great deal more failure is the result of an excess of caution than of bold experimentation with new ideas. The frontiers of the kingdom of God were never advanced by men and women of caution.

—Oswald Sanders

You never know how much you really believe anything until its truth or falsehood becomes a matter of life or death to you.

—C. S. Lewis

When Abram was called out of Ur with these words of commission—

The LORD had said to Abram, "Leave your country, your people and your father's household and go to the land I will show you.

"I will make you into a great nation
 and I will bless you;
I will make your name great,
 and you will be a blessing." (Gen. 12:1–2)

—he responded in an act of obedience that quite literally altered the course of history. This was surely one of the most momentous and decisive moments in the history of world redemption. But it was not an act taken dispassionately, for it must have involved significant risk and enormous amounts of courage to pull off. In fact, Abram was being called by a deity, who at that point in his experience must have been to him a Great Mystery. And he was called to step out on an uncertain journey into a great unknown.

This took a leap of faith to be sure, but it is also a near perfect example of what we call the *faith of leap*. All the elements explored in this book—risk, adventure, courage, and the implications for church, discipleship, mission, and the self—are in some seminal way contained, as well as demonstrated, in Abraham's courageous response to God.

Think of it this way: Abram's somewhat "unbalanced" action put him (as well as his rather large household) at serious risk. At the very least, it dislocated him from his land, severed him from the familiar comfort of kith and kin, and resulted in a dangerous, lifelong journey that involved what can only be called open-ended adventure and discovery. It was a truly existential act. It was a leap of faith to be sure, but it also led to a life of faithfulness that has set the parameters of how we as God's people ought to understand what it is to live a life pleasing to God.

The result is that we all now take our cue from Abraham. Paul even says it is the Abrahamic type of faith that is required to access the promises of God in the first place. It is precisely this type of risk-embracing, adventure-engaging, courageous faith in God that justifies. Without it we cannot even be saved, let alone live the Christian life (see, for example, Rom. 4; Gal. 3). It is not superfluous to the Christian life; we are saved by faith, but we are also called to continue living by the same faith (Rom. 1:16–17; Eph. 2:8–10).

When Abraham acted in response to God's command, and stayed the course in the open-ended adventure that followed, he gave us faith's archetypal human expression. It is called "faithfulness" in the Scriptures themselves, and it forms the basis of what the Bible understands as true heroism—it is for good reason that Abram was later renamed Abraham, the father of the faithful.

Abraham's type of faith (the *faith of leap*) sets the standard for subsequent acts of biblical heroism. For instance, it took a similar faith of leap for Peter to immediately drop his fishing nets and follow Jesus in Matthew 4, and later to launch himself from a boat in the midst of a windstorm, toward the ghostlike figure of Jesus in the middle of the Sea of Galilee in Matthew 14. Likewise, Paul's missionary journeys into the unknown are truly *Abrahamic* and have set a high standard for all Christian discipleship ever since. So too all the other acts of faith, by countless saints, that have demonstrated courage, conviction, and the capacity to risk all for God.

If you are reading this book, chances are that you have already taken the leap of saving faith, but like all who are called to follow Jesus, you are required to live with the faith of leap. All disciples of Jesus (not just a select few) are called to an ongoing, risky, actional, extravagant way of life—a life resonant with that distinctly wild—and yes, *Christlike*—faithfulness of their Lord and Master. This is the faith that is willing to leap into service of his unfurling reign in this world, believing that by so doing we are partnering with him in a cosmic project for the regeneration of all things, far and away more amazing than anything we could have conceived of ourselves.

From the Leap of Faith to the Faith of Leap

Most of us scan the news every day, but have you ever considered why we actually do this? What draws us back to the television news channels or the daily newspaper or the myriad online news services day after day, night after night? Our first response might be that we are simply keeping up with what's going on in the world, that we want to be able to engage in informed conversation with others. But that can't fully explain our fascination with the unfolding of events nor the enormous amounts of money and media resources put into capturing and channeling that news to information-hungry audiences around the world.

Perhaps we follow the news out of an almost mysterious sense that all of life is somehow interconnected, and that events that happen across the world can, and often do, have global, and sometimes very personal, significance. After all, September 11, although it happened in New York, Washington, and the countryside of Pennsylvania, was global in impact. While it changed the world, it also impacted us very personally as well. In many ways the news involves the unfolding of the human story of which *I* am, *we* are, a fundamental part. Life, including our corporate life, is marvelously intertwined and open-ended. Who knows what will happen next?

For good or for ill, we are all players in the living drama going on around us. God has designed us as decision makers in his very image, as agents of the kingdom, not only to partake in history, but to prayerfully shape and direct it in his name as a true act of worship.[1] And the part we play will depend largely on a clear sense of our mission, on the level of intentionality in what we do, and on the fortitude and integrity with which we do it. In short, it will depend on our desire to muster the faith of leap. It will also depend on the guide(s) that we follow in that endeavor.

This idea—that we all have our parts to play in a grand unfolding story—is variously portrayed by Tolkien's marvelous characters in the Lord of the Rings trilogy. One particularly wise character, Samwise Gamgee, proves his uncomplicated genius by rightly locating his and Frodo's plight within a larger, now unfolding adventure, the outcome of which no one could predict. Whilst approaching Mordor, and resigned to their common fate and calling, he says to Frodo,

> The brave things in the old tales and songs, Mr. Frodo, *adventures* as I used to call them. I used to think that they were things the wonderful folk of the stories went out and looked for because they wanted them, because they were exciting and life was a bit dull, a kind of sport, as you might say. But that's not the way of it with the tales that really mattered, or the ones that stay in the mind. Folk seem to have been just landed in them, usually—their paths were laid that way, as you put it. But I expect they had lots of chances, like us, of turning back, only they didn't. And if they had, we shouldn't know, because they'd have been forgotten. We hear about those as just went on—and not all to a good end, mind you; at least not to what folk inside a story and not outside it call a good end. You know, coming home, and finding things all right, though not quite the same—like old Mr. Bilbo. But those aren't always the best tales to hear, though they may be the best tales to get landed in! I wonder what sort of a tale we've fallen into?[2]

Such stories are later remembered, Sam observes, because their characters—usually against their own wishes—find themselves embarking upon a quest, a mission, the outcome of which involves something immensely larger and more important than their own personal comfort and happiness. Tolkien understood that a quest is never a matter of one's own desire but rather of one's calling. For instance, in the trilogy, Frodo frequently questions why he has been *chosen* for this utterly dreadful task. But however he might struggle to articulate it, he does feel *called*, he feels profoundly obligated, to continue his particular mission (his "errand," as he calls it) in spite of the horrendous situations in which he continues to find himself.[3]

And remember, Frodo and his friends have no guarantee, perhaps not even the likelihood, that the quest will succeed. In fact, they seem to be constantly moving *toward* danger, never away from it toward any kind of permanent safety. They seem to constantly inhabit the liminal space: *Liminality* is the term we use to describe a threshold experience. It is composed of any or a combination of danger, marginality, disorientation, or ordeal and tends to create a space that is neither here nor there, a transitional stage between what was and what is to come. As a result, it is experienced as a place of discomfort and agitation that requires us to endure and push into what is to come. And it describes perfectly the experience of Frodo and his companions in the Lord of the Rings stories.

Liminality, it seems, is the true context of a quest. To remind Frodo of the radical open-endedness of the journey, his uncle Bilbo composed a "walking song" to give him courage and determination when he will be sorely tempted to veer off the Road.

> The Road goes ever on and on
>   Down from the door where it began.
> Now far ahead the Road has gone,
>   And I must follow, if I can,
> Pursuing it with weary feet,
>   Until it joins some larger way,
> Where many paths and errands meet,
>   And whither then? I cannot say.[4]

The Fellowship's quest to destroy the Ring—having no guarantee of success but rather an immense likelihood of failure—is not unlike any true quest of life, and perhaps especially true for the disciple and for Christian community. Tolkien, speaking through Bilbo here, proposes the idea that we all have an "errand"—a unique mission and purpose—that far from being some artificial adventure (the kind one experiences in Disneyland) takes us to the heart of the meaning of one's life. And whether we like it or not, we are all on a journey, a Quest if you will, every day of our lives, and the path we must take is full of perils, and our destiny can never be predicted in advance. As Legolas says, "Few can foresee whither their road will lead them, till they come to its end." And, "the question—and thus the Quest—concerns *how* we shall travel the road and whether we shall complete our errand."[5] And for disciples of Jesus, like the Fellowship of the Ring, the struggle for the good against the evil requires nothing less than everything—the giving up of our lives— whether sooner or later, whether bitterly or graciously, whether by happenstance or intention.

We think that Tolkien is spot on here. He mythically portrays for us the Christian story and the Quest of the church. As people caught up in the Jesus story, we can interpret life truly only from within a larger gospel narrative where we all play a part in the constant unfolding of God's purposes in his world. We are explicitly warned that there can be no final respite until we reach our final Sabbath rest (Heb. 4:1–11), and although there will, thankfully, be wonderful resting places along the way, these we can never settle in for too long. We rest only to be strengthened for the Journey.

As it happens, we are still in the middle of an open-ended story of what Jesus is doing in the world, and the book of Acts must continue to be written by Christians in every age and context. We are the people of the ultimate Quest—we are on a wild, and sometimes dangerous, adventure to save the world. This is our story and our song.

The End of the Beginning

As Jesus's people, we are part of a story that originated in the eternal heart of God, was carried out through the redemptive mission of the Son, and continues in the sending of the Holy Spirit and in the commissioning of the church in the power of that Spirit. It's a story that has unfolded first through Israel but now further extends itself through the messianic movement that Jesus started. But the biblical people of God, be they Israel or early church, far from being the end of the story, are rather the "end of the beginning." They just got the whole thing started—we now carry the baton. But they witness to us, calling us to remain true to the Quest. And so we joyfully continue, perhaps even bring to completion, the Mission with the same kind of faithfulness and integrity that our biblical forebears brought to the task.

We are the people born of the *missio Dei*. This means that the church is a result of the missionary activity of God and not the producer of it. The church is therefore defined by its mission and not the other way around. And this mission of redemption is not yet fulfilled; therefore, we are still on the Journey. As in our previous books, we say that Christology (our primary theology) determines Missiology (our purpose and function), which in turn determines Ecclesiology (the forms and expressions of the church).[6] We are the missional people of God, and we have a job to accomplish that only we, as Jesus's people, can do.

The church doesn't *have* an agenda; it *is* the agenda. The church doesn't *have* a missional strategy; it *is* the missional strategy. Therefore, to be the church as we are meant to be is of utmost missional importance in our day. But herein lies the rub: Christianity has been on a long-term trend of decline in every Western cultural context that we can identify. Part of the reason is that we now live in a post-Christian, post-Christendom world—the result is that seventeen centuries of "Western church" have effectively inoculated our culture against the gospel.

British missiologist Stuart Murray defines post-Christendom as

the culture that emerges as the Christian faith loses coherence within a society that has been definitively shaped by the Christian story and as the institutions that have been developed to express Christian convictions decline in influence.[7]

He notes some significant shifts that have massive consequences for how we go about church and mission as post-Christendom effects the following transitions:

From the centre to margins: in Christendom the Christian story and the churches were central, but in post-Christendom these are marginal.

From majority to minority: in Christendom Christians comprised the (often overwhelming) majority, but in post-Christendom we are a minority.

From settlers to sojourners: in Christendom Christians felt at home in a culture shaped by our story, but in post-Christendom we are aliens, exiles, and pilgrims in a culture where we no longer feel at home.

From privilege to plurality: in Christendom Christians enjoyed many privileges, but in post-Christendom we are one community among many in a plural society.

From control to witness: in Christendom churches could exert control over society, but in post-Christendom we exercise influence only through witnessing to our story and its implications.

From maintenance to mission: in Christendom the emphasis was on maintaining a supposedly Christian status quo, but in post-Christendom it is on mission within a contested environment.

From institution to movement: in Christendom churches operated mainly in institutional mode, but in post-Christendom we must again become a Christian movement.[8]

Our situation has fundamentally changed, and we must now find ways to adapt or to simply continue on the way of decline. In our opinion, though, far from representing a defeat of the gospel, this situation—which is just beginning to dawn upon the consciousness of church leaders in the United States—gives us a wonderful opportunity to return to basics and recalibrate back beyond the highly institutionalized, overly stylized forms of church that have currently imprisoned our imaginations. The time is ripe to (re)discover a much more potent and theologically consistent understanding of ourselves. It's a time to journey in our minds and hearts, to find a better way to be the good news people of God that Jesus designed us to be. The Christian community, at least as Jesus intended it, is one of the most exciting aspects of the gospel experience: the church is the frontier of the kingdom, the place

where *it* all happens, where love lives, where the living witness to
our Lord must take place.

Casting Off in the Midst of Crisis

If we take Jesus's founding words as seriously as he actually intended
("And I tell you that you are Peter, and on this rock I will build my
church, and the gates of Hades will not overcome it. I will give you the
keys of the kingdom of heaven," Matt.16:18–19; see also 28:18–20),
then we have to admit that we have been in a Rip Van Winklesque
slumber for way too long already. We have been whacked out by the
dreaded opiate of "religion," and as a result we have ended up with
something significantly less than a biblical experience of church.

But crisis is in some real sense normative for the church of Jesus,
because it is there where we are most authentic. David Bosch, one of
our great guides in the twentieth century, elaborates on the words of
another great missiologist, Hendrik Kraemer, when he says,

> It is . . . normal for Christians to live in a situation of crisis. . . .
> "Strictly speaking, one ought to say that the Church is always in
> a state of crisis and that its greatest shortcoming is that it is only
> occasionally aware of it." This ought to be the case . . . because of
> "the abiding tension between (the church's) essential nature and its
> empirical condition." . . . The church "has always needed apparent
> failure and suffering in order to become fully alive to its real nature
> and mission." . . . And for many centuries the church has suffered so
> little and has been led to believe that it was a success. . . .
> *Let us also know that to encounter crisis is to encounter the pos-
> sibility of truly being the church.*[9]

Crisis is no bad thing. In fact it's an opportunity to rediscover the
adventurous church. And the signs are good: it seems to us that the
church in the United States is indeed beginning to rise to the challenge, although we have just put our foot to that road again—and
who knows where it will take us. We will have to take risks, to chance
failure, to be willing to walk away from the familiar paths that have
brought us to this point. It is clear that simply opting for more of
the same is not going to resolve our problems. We must be willing

to dream again, to innovate, and to risk the rejection of peers who think that the status quo is sufficient to the task. The church should be one of the most adventurous places on earth—the locus of all quest, the highly adaptive Jesus community at the very forefront of what God is doing in the world. But let's be honest—this is not the case with the church-as-we-know-it.

It's time to move, to cast off from safe shores, and take a journey again! The church as an expression, perhaps the most concentrated expression, of the kingdom of God on earth should be a fully God-alive, dynamic, adventurous, world-transforming agency.

We love this quote, ascribed to Catholic theologian Hans Küng, because it highlights our intrinsic need for adventure and innovation:

> A church which pitches its tents without constantly looking out for new horizons, which does not continually strike camp, is being untrue to its calling. . . . [We must] play down our longing for certainty, accept what is risky, live by improvisation and experiment.[10]

To do this, to rediscover church as missional adventure, we will have to start by *reJesusing* the church[11]—we need to be willing to factor Jesus, the wild Lord (his life, teachings, ministry, salvation work), back into the equation of church—to become disciples *on the Way*. And in terms of the church, we will need to rediscover the meaning of the word *movement* and relinquish being administrators of a stifling status quo, or worse, purveyors of fine religion. If we do this, we will experience spiritual renewal, the burning fire, and the accompanying gravitas that pervaded the New Testament church.

To end this introduction where we started—all who have seen the Lord of the Rings movies, or better, have read the books, will quickly recognize that Tolkien's work is imbued with the mystical sense that life is a mission that carries us beyond that which is familiar. On the Road, wherever it might take us, even small acts have grand possible consequences. As Baylor University professor Ralph Wood says,

> To get out of bed, to answer the phone, to respond to a knock at the door, to open a letter—such everyday deeds are freighted, willy-nilly, with eternal consequence. From the greatest to the smallest acts of either courage or cowardice, we travel irresistibly on the path toward ultimate joy or final ruin.[12]

Wood then quotes Tolkein directly:

> [Bilbo] used often to say that there was only one Road; that it was like a great river: its springs are at every doorstep, and every path is its tributary. "It's a dangerous business, Frodo, going out of your door," he used to say. "You step into the Road, and if you don't keep your feet, there's no knowing where you might be swept off to."[13]

According to Tolkien, we can "keep our feet"—i.e., we can avoid being swept away to the death that comes from having failed our mission—only so long as we have a sure sense of where we are supposed to be going and how we may rightly arrive there.

That we are all, individually or corporately, on a mission emanating from the heart of God is clear and unavoidable—there is, biblically speaking, no such thing as a nonmissional church or disciple. And because we *are* that, we are part of the unfolding of the Story, and we must play our part and do it faithfully. To take ourselves out of the Quest is to block the purposes of the *missio Dei* as it flows through us, and is therefore blatant unfaithfulness to God and disloyalty to the grandest of Causes.

To keep our feet on the Adventure, however, will require staying close to our Founder and Leader, who is himself the Way, the Truth, and the Life, the Alpha and Omega. He is well able to define, keep, shape, and guide us into the future of the kingdom of God, because he is also the King.

1

The Spirit's Edge

Putting Adventure Back into the Venture

I should have been a true and passionate Christian. The Adventurer. But now I live in 1924, and the Christian venture is done. The adventure is gone out of Christianity. We must start on a new venture towards God.

—D. H. Lawrence

It is the unknown that defines our existence. We are constantly seeking, not just for answers to our questions, but for new questions. We are explorers.

—Ben Cisco, *Star Trek: Deep Space Nine*

As many readers well know, the novelist D. H. Lawrence was no friend of the church. He believed that the repressive morality of Christianity was the source of much of the social and political disintegration of Western Europe in the early twentieth century. Writing in 1924, he claimed that any sense of daring or adventure had been leached from Christianity, leaving only the brittle shell of suppression and safe respectability—Christianity, in his opinion, was a spent force.

While we might agree with aspects of his diagnosis, we are certainly at odds with his prognosis. Lawrence saw no hope for re-energizing the adventureless church of his day, but we are not at all pessimistic. Indeed, we believe that twenty-first-century Christians are yearning to see the adventure put back into Christianity, into the relationship with the living God—where it rightly belongs. Lawrence's mistaken answer was to invoke some kind of gnostic spirituality, involving a reconnection with the purifying forces of nature. Whatever the error of his personal choice, he wrote movingly of fresh energy beyond institutional forms of religion. We do well to heed the power of these words:

> When we get out of the glass bottles of our ego,
> and when we escape like squirrels turning in the
> cages of our personality
> and get into the forests again,
> we shall shiver with cold and fright
> but things will happen to us
> so that we don't know ourselves.
>
> Cool, unlying life will rush in,
> and passion will make our bodies taut with power,
> we shall stamp our feet with new power
> and old things will fall down,
> we shall laugh, and institutions will curl up like
> burnt paper.[1]

It might be tempting for Christian readers to reject this as poetic mumbo jumbo, but we do so at our peril. What Lawrence was yearning for, and what we equally yearn for, was that sense of *life*, fully lived and completely free from the cramping influence of various controlling institutionalisms.

The "cool, unlying life" that Lawrence wanted to rush in on him is the very thing that Jesus offers his followers. This life is ours not through the purifying effects of nature, but by the purifying death and resurrection of Jesus. It is our faith in him that brings life, and with such life the followers of Jesus will "stamp our feet with new power and old things will fall down."

The writer of Hebrews celebrates this very power—a power derived from the risen Christ, a power that is testified to by that great collection of witnesses, the faithful ones. In each case, the heroes he brings forth as evidence of faith's redemptive power are those who resisted the powers of their day and embraced the very adventure Lawrence so deeply desires.

Hebrews is a song about faith as an adventure, and chapter 12 is its chorus, resounding with stories of historical faithfulness. While Lawrence thought life could be found outside human society, the writer of Hebrews tells us that it is in the very line or genealogy of the faithful ones that such life can be found with Jesus at its center.

It is not dissimilar to that found in Tolkien's classic, *The Lord of the Rings*. What we find in our heroes and martyrs is a living witness (the famous "cloud" of Heb. 12:1) to the fact that the true life of faith can only be nobly inspired and rightly lived if one takes it on bravely and gallantly, as something of a grand adventure in which we set out into an unknown country to face many a danger, to meet many a joy, to find many a comrade, to win and lose many a battle.

Far from being incidental to the life of faith, the element of adventure is as intrinsic to discipleship and community as Jesus designed it to be. When we embrace liminality—that in-between, discomforting place described earlier—and engage it head-on, we discover the truest sense of adventure. In fact, we will argue, without the adventure we lose the necessary pathos by which we can truly understand the human situation and the meaning of the church. The loss of spiritual adventure produces a somewhat distorted sense of what it means to be in the Way of Jesus—we become bored Christians acquiescing to the lame dictates of a mediocre life, sensing that we are missing out on something important but not willing to pay the price to do anything about it. This is an inauthentic place for any follower of Jesus to be, and nothing could be further from the type of community that Jesus envisioned his church to become.

So we will investigate the dynamics of courage, adventure, mission, and risk—all elements in what we want to put under the general category of "liminality"—and to explore why they are crucial to a genuinely *biblical* Christianity. But we do so not because we are adrenaline junkies (we are not), but because we believe that there is no way back to radical discipleship and an authentic experience of church without it. Liminality has direct implications for our understanding of theology, philosophy, literature, discipleship, psychology, society, and community.

The Elements of a Liminal Life

The poet T. S. Eliot suggested that the end of all exploring was to arrive where we began and to know the place for the first time. To learn, to grow, to mature, requires a journey from where we are now. And it is only after journeys of exploration that we will return to our most basic of beliefs and really know them personally. Without such movement there can be no real learning, development, or maturity. Whatever knowledge we might retain in the safe, self-protective space will end up being merely secondhand, dangerously depersonalized and depersonalizing data—nothing close to the way the Bible sees faith.

Living Adventurously

By definition, an *adventure* is a journey with an uncertain outcome. Radical open-endedness has always characterized the human experience, but there can be no doubt it definitely describes our situation in the twenty-first century. We live in an age of considerable uncertainty—who knows what five, ten, twenty years will bring? The combination of climate change, revolutionary technologies, and massive geopolitical shifts alone is enough to cause overwhelming excitement or anxiety. Then add all the other factors that come into the mix. Because of this global uncertainty, the visionary and the adventurous amongst us will get to shape the future of the twenty-first century—the church included.

Adventure is an attitude we must apply to the day-to-day obstacles of life—facing new challenges, seizing new opportunities, testing our resources against the unknown, and in the process, discovering our own unique potential as God's people. Adventure does not consist in something won or lost, enjoyed or endured. Rather, it is the very rhythm of life itself, and acknowledging this transforms mere experience into an adventure. If missional discipleship and community have anything to say to us, it is to call us to precisely this kind of life.

It is not an overstatement to summarize Jesus's work on earth as that of starting an adventure. Thus we follow Jesus to the extent that we are part of the adventure he started. We fail to follow him to the extent that we check out of this divine drama, this adventure of mission. Note the word *began* in the following verse from Acts: "In my former book, Theophilus, I wrote about all that Jesus began to do and to teach" (1:1). He began it; our job is to keep it going.

To follow Jesus fundamentally changes the way we view our lives, the world, and our roles within it. To love God and others opens us up to the full possibilities of life and requires that we enter on a journey in which he leads us into our future. So in many ways it is a matter of perspective—how we perceive our world and our role within it. Or as G. K. Chesterton rightly observed, "An adventure is only an inconvenience rightly considered. An inconvenience is an adventure wrongly considered." Much depends on how we perceive life—as threat or opportunity.

We have already referred to the idea of adventure being something of an open-ended journey. It is important to understand what this means and see how it sheds light on the challenges facing Christianity in the twenty-first century. We don't believe that adventure is simply a vacation, a pilgrimage, or an ordinary journey. In fact, as Samwise Gamgee points out, often we do not choose to undertake an adventure. It chooses us.

Our preferences for stability and security blind us to the opportunities for adventure when they present themselves. Adventures are events, dramas, and stories into which individuals and communities are swept up, their end uncertain and their plot indecipherable. In an adventure, we become players in a larger drama that unfolds as we go. However, there is no real control over the beginning or end of the journey—we must simply choose to see it through or to opt out. And while we cannot fully predict where the adventure will take us, we do get to shape and direct the final outcomes through our action or nonaction. Because of all this, an adventure fully engages the adventurer; it is packed with risk and reward, uncertainty and vindication, threat and promise.

All this describes life itself. Life, when viewed as existing between the events of birth and death, and focused to a point, can also be perceived as a journey, an adventure, with a start and an end. Bringing

31

the "religious" element into the equation only massively heightens this sense of adventure.[2] In Christ, our actions have eternal consequences, and even the least of us can become spiritual heroes. When Christians lose sight that we live *sub specie aeternitatis*—under the aspect of eternity—life loses its connection to the grand enfolding narrative, and with that, our sense of purpose and our role in the story, our *heroism* as it were, is diminished. This reminds one of Kierkegaard's "knight of faith"—someone who risks all to pursue that which is of infinite, eternal worth.

But adventurers do not only traverse boundaries by themselves—they usually travel with others, and together they return from their adventures with new stories, fresh revelations, and novel perspectives from afar, which in turn change the environment of their homecoming.

It is not hard to see how being incorporated into the gospel story involves us in a grand adventure, where, following the Spirit, we all get to participate with what God is doing in the world. We are all "players" that shape the outcomes through our active involvement with the story as it unfolds through our lives. And given the personal cost of such involvement, many would rather opt out, preferring the static life of middle-class respectability to the wild and erratic undertaking of following Jesus. So we become nostalgic and sentimental, wistfully reflecting on the days of our youthful adventures, feeding off fading memory rather than living in current experience, living in an idealized past rather than facing God's future. And the biggest mistake in doing this is mistaking this nostalgia for security in God.

In light of God's claim over our lives, personal security is all an illusion. As Helen Keller observed, "Security is mostly a superstition. It does not exist in nature, nor do the children of men as a whole experience it. Avoiding danger is no safer in the long run than outright exposure. Life is either a daring adventure or nothing."[3]

C. S. Lewis addressed this matter of perspective in his characteristically brilliant way during his talk to a group of would-be university students at the beginning of the Second World War.

> I think it important to try and see the present calamity in a true perspective. The war creates no absolutely new situation: it simply aggravates the permanent human situation so that we can no longer

ignore it. Human life has always been lived on the edge of the precipice. Human culture has always had to exist under the shadow of something infinitely more important than itself. If men had postponed the search for knowledge and beauty until they were secure, the search would never have begun. We are mistaken when we compare war with "normal life." Life has never been normal.[4]

When our need for security becomes obsessive, we remove ourselves from the journey of discipleship. By then we have given in to insecurity, and the price is a high one—it becomes an enslaving idol. Making ourselves ever more secure will not keep the fear of insecurity from becoming a possessive demon. The hold of the idol can be broken only by acting directly against it. As French philosopher Jacques Ellul said, "There is an exact equilibrium. The more security and guarantees we want against things, the less free we are. Tyrants are not to be feared today, but our own frantic need of security is. Freedom inevitably means insecurity and responsibility."[5] To use the biblical imagery, we must live in the fear of the Lord and strive against the forces of death. Bunkering down in some sort of false, idolatrous security can only hinder our cause, not advance it.

In this world, there is no such thing as a sure thing. We cannot even control the outcome of a single day. When we think we are in control, we have only bought an illusion. Even if all our efforts go well, the details and all kinds of things that transpire as well as the outcomes will probably be different from what we originally intended anyhow. It's just the way it is: we can't control as much as we'd like to suppose.

And so we must go about our pursuits, not resting in some false sense of material security, but responding with faith and trust in Jesus to the onrush of events. We Christians are the great adventurers of the earth, and our lives are crisscrossed everywhere by the characteristics of true adventure. But we only now and then become aware of this fact when something happens to remind us that we are indeed involved in something larger than our self-enclosed concerns—only then does our sense of being on an "adventure" arise. But it is there whether we recognize it or not, and our capacity to "see" this will make the difference of whether we live faithfully or not.

33

Courage for the Journey

To be the liminal church that Jesus designed takes real courage. C. S. Lewis's fictional demon Screwtape advises his nephew Wormwood on the virtue of courage, or the lack thereof:

> In peace we can make many of them [humans] ignore good and evil entirely; in danger, the issue is forced upon them in a guise to which even we cannot blind them. There is here a cruel dilemma before us. If we promoted justice and charity among men, we should be playing directly into the Enemy's hands; but if we guide them to the opposite behaviour, this sooner or later produces (for He permits it to produce) a war or a revolution, and the undisguisable issue of cowardice or courage awakes thousands of men from moral stupor. *This, indeed, is probably one of the Enemy's* [God's] *motives for creating a dangerous world—a world in which moral issues really come to the point.* He sees as well as you do *that courage is not simply one of the virtues, but the form of every virtue at the testing point*, which means, at the point of highest reality. A chastity or honesty, or mercy, which yields to danger will be chaste or honest or merciful only on conditions. Pilate was merciful till it became risky.[6]

Listen carefully to what is being said here: Lewis is suggesting that courage is the greatest of all virtues, because unless a person possesses that virtue, they have no real capacity for preserving any of the others when it really matters. As he indicates, Pilate was merciful only *until* it became risky for him to be so. Self-interest and security kicked in and effectively expelled mercy at the point where he was called to actually be merciful. Likewise, people tend to be obedient only up to the point of where it costs them. But this is actually what it means to be cowards—to be unwilling to confront a reasonable degree of fear and anxiety when it matters most.

To live faithfully in this "dangerous world" in which we are called to be the church requires real courage. As theologian Scott Bader-Saye recently wrote, "Courage is the capacity to do what is right and good in the face of fear. We become courageous when we learn to live for something that is more important than our own safety."[7]

And so when we embrace our calling as courageous adventurers, what needs to be borne in mind? Here are some pointers for would-be voyagers:

1. You cannot really take the risks of obedience if you are not rightly loving the Father, through Jesus, in the power of the Spirit. Adventurous disciples and churches maintain the essential God-relationship by whatever means available.
2. While courage is the antithesis of fear, biblical courage readily embraces the fear of God and refuses the fear of man. To fear God is to respect that which is ultimate and most important, giving us a right perspective and keeping us faithfully on the road. Even death in Jesus's cause is only the beginning of even greater things in God. Remember the martyrs and their witness to us.
3. To obey God is often countercultural and counterintuitive, and it requires risk by daring to fly in the face of convention and even of opposition. Unless we are renewing our perspectives with a transcendent biblical perspective (Rom. 12:1–3), we'll probably buckle under the pressure and give way to the ambient call of the world.
4. Recognize that God is the sovereign King who is directing all things to a final goal when he will be all in all (1 Cor. 15:28). At one point or another, each of us will think that this is not the case, so we have to constantly remind each other of this truth.
5. Courage finds its greatest expression in love and sacrifice. It is that point where we can be sure we are in the faith (1 John 3). When we really love, consistently and in Jesus's name, we are being as courageous as we are ever expected to be.

Embracing Risk

When we began our research into the link between adventure, God, and the church, we found that no sustained academic work had been previously written on the subject. Books that explore a theology of risk, adventure, and courage simply do not exist. This is surprising, given the surfeit of material written on more peripheral theological matters, and it is a huge indicator of how lackluster, nonmissional, and passive our thinking about the Trinity, church, and discipleship have become.

The closest we could find to a theology of risk comes from the controversial area of "open theism," a theological movement that has developed within evangelical and post-evangelical Protestant Christianity in response to the infusion of Hellenistic ideas into Western Christian theology. Examples of such a fusion of ideas within classical theism are, among others, the teaching that God is immutable (unmoving/unchangeable), impassible (without passion/emotion), and timeless (in the sense of completely ahistorical). Furthermore it asserts that God fully predetermines the future; thus, humanity does not have free will, or if free, we are free only within the highly conditioned boundaries of God's predetermining will and action. Open theists reject this "closed view of God" and argue that these attributes do not belong to the God of the Bible and are at odds with personhood (and the human reflection and image of God) in general.[8]

It is beyond our scope and expertise to present or even critique this debate; we simply note here that while open theism is willing to admit that risk happens both within God and to God, classical theism seems to exclude this on principle.

To our minds at least, the freedom and contingency that God grants to his creation must in some way imply risk; otherwise, the concept of freedom has no inherent reality and meaning. For instance, to love in any sense of the word means choosing to be open in some sense to pain and loss, and therefore risk. And it does appear that the God of Revelation loves in this way: he feels very deeply the lostness of his creation. It also recognizes that in the incarnation, God must have taken some significant risk related to the humanity of Jesus because to be truly human means to be subject to some form of finitude, to lack the comprehensive vision, power, and knowledge that is required to make risk-free choices. The early church considered heresy anything that diminished the authentic humanity of Jesus (e.g., docetism, gnosticism, etc.) and rightly so. Our understanding of the incarnation and the salvation gained through Jesus is at stake here.

Furthermore, it seems correct to say that God took something of a risk in handing over his mission to the all-too-sinful human beings who were the original disciples—and all the sinful disciples beyond them. We wonder what Jesus must have been thinking on the cross, when all but a few powerless women had completely abandoned him. Did he wonder if love alone was enough to draw them back into discipleship? The noncoercive love of the cross necessitated a genuinely human response of willing obedience from his disciples. Given our predispositions to rebellion and idolatry, it is entirely conceivable that history could have gone in a completely different, indeed totally disastrous, direction if the original disciples hadn't plucked up the internal courage to follow Jesus no matter where. They took on the adventure of discipleship in response to the risky love that God had bestowed upon them in Jesus. There were no risk-free scenarios here, no guarantees that they would make the right choices. If this is not the case, then we are not human precisely at the point where we must be most completely human: in freely offering our lives back to God in love and adoration. This assumes that it might not have been so, or else the choice for Jesus is no choice at all.

Given the narrative structure of the Bible, we can also state that God is an adventurer. He is the subject of a living Story still being told. He extends himself, actively engaging in all sorts of historical events—war, peace, judgment, redemption, salvation, and so forth. He feels deeply the events of the world. The Bible is full of phrases that describe God's pathos arising from his involvement in human history. He initiates events; he responds to human concerns; he sings, weeps, cajoles, and gets angry. Furthermore, in response to the sinful human condition, he "sends" his Son and Spirit on a (still ongoing) mission to redeem the world.

But any theology of adventure must also take eschatology seriously. Indeed, it is inherent in any attempt to comprehend God and the teachings of the Bible. Take eschatology out of the equation and you end up with a completely distorted view of the biblical revelation. In fact, it can't be understood at all.

When we look into the nature of eschatology, we will find a theological structure that gives us a conceptual framework within which to understand the ongoing adventure of the church. Even a cursory reading of the book of Revelation gives us a sense of the ultimate meaning of events and our role within them. Here we see the crashing in of the kingdom of God, creating urgency, demanding change, calling us forward to a vision of what will be when the Messiah returns. Just as the Pevensie children find themselves in the middle of a war

① Part of theology concerned w/ death, judgement, & final destiny of soul & humankind

37

when in Narnia, those who repent and turn to Jesus are automatically co-opted into the revolution that he started. The kingdom of God is a crash-bang opera: the King is dramatic, demanding, and unavoidable.

But that's not the whole truth about the kingdom. It also intrudes into our world and works on us secretly and subversively—like yeast working its way through dough, like seeds stealthily growing into trees, like wheat growing quietly in a field. It is present right here, right now, and yet needs to be completely fulfilled, and sometimes one can be forgiven for thinking that it had never arrived at all. But we Christians know that it has. It is our D-day to the ever-encroaching V-day. The war is won in Jesus's life, death, and resurrection, but there are still many battles to be fought. This subversive kingdom undermines the status quo, creates spiritual unrest, breaks hard hearts, and instills righteousness. Like pilgrims in a strange land, we are called to the Journey, to be great adventurers, the eschatological people of God. We are secret agents; we are in the middle of an assignment, engaged on that grand Adventure.

Eschatology therefore not only gives us an external framework to understand the adventure of the church but provides us with an inbuilt theological mechanism that creates a constant, unrelenting, deeply internalized theological pressure on the community of faith. This in itself provides us with an internal liminality, because it urgently presses us toward adaptation to a vision of what can be and is not yet. When our life here strikes us as a mere preliminary phase in the fulfillment of eternal destinies, when we have no home but merely a temporary asylum on earth, we get the feeling that life as a whole is an adventure.[9] Vision changes us, but a kingdom vision changes *everything*.

The "not yet" aspect of the kingdom of God means that the Acts of the Apostles is still being written by the church in every age, including the contemporary one. Not in the way that it is canonical and authoritative to be sure, but nonetheless every bit as valid and authentic as the early church. The revolution of Jesus marches on—the job is not yet complete—and we remain in the ranks of those who have heeded the call. As Martin Luther suggested, the church should live its life as if Jesus died yesterday, rose from the dead today, and is coming back tomorrow.

Mission as a Liminal Space

We mentioned earlier that we believe that mission is one of the elements of liminality. By that we mean that mission, by its very nature, creates the conditions of liminality. If mission involves alerting others to the universal reign of God through Christ,[10] then we need to recognize that this reign is not only disputed, it is rejected by the vast majority of people—this alone puts us at odds with what is considered real and normal. Furthermore, while the kingdom has been inaugurated in the incarnation, death, and resurrection of Jesus (it is full, complete, and irreversible), it is not yet fully consummated, and so we live in an in-between time, a time after its inauguration and before its completion in the return of Christ. By its very nature then, mission (especially evangelistic mission) is a liminal activity. It sits between what is and what is to come.

Jesus himself referred to us being "in the world but not of the world" (John 17:11, 16), as good a liminal expression as you'll find. We don't belong in the world as it is now. Our destiny lies in the world to come, but like Frodo and his companion in the Lord of the Rings, we press on in this journey, knowing our function here is not merely to endure but to effect change in Jesus's name as commanded by the King whose reign we announce and demonstrate.

But more than this, there is a sense of mission as a liminal activity when brave followers of King Jesus step out of the supposedly safe haven of the church into the world to love and serve others as a demonstration of his reign and to share the good news of that reign with them. Mission is risky, requiring us to step into the unknown with little more than a commitment to the vision of what Jesus wants from his world.

Therefore, missional living can only be lived out in whichever liminal state the church finds itself and requires a sense of risk and adventure to ensure its success.

Cultivating a Holy Urgency

One of the key benefits of putting a theology of adventure back into our venture of church is that it creates a right sense of holy urgency needed for us to learn and adapt to changing conditions. Our best eschatology teaches us that there is no time when this has been more important than right now. Spiritual urgency, the kind which imbues the prophetic writings, involves a heightened sense of spiritual intelligence combined with passion to focus the mind as fully as possible on the issues and challenges at hand.

A sense of holy urgency is vital to church life because it creates the right sense of immediacy to provoke holy action. It is through holy urgency that we overcome unholy complacency. When imbued with an appropriate sense of urgency, people and churches become alert and proactive, seeking information relative to development and success of their mission. In other words, they become a learning organization—highly adaptive and responsive to the changing conditions around them.

John Kotter, Professor of Leadership Emeritus at Harvard Business School and the author of several books on leadership and change, enumerates in his landmark book *Leading Change* eight necessary steps for bringing significant and lasting change to an organization.[11] The first of these steps is to create a sense of urgency and lace it throughout the organization. Over the years, as he further studied change in organizations, he came to the conclusion that the lack of a sense of urgency accounted for 70 percent of all major change efforts failing or being completed significantly behind schedule or over budget. So, sensing the strategic nature of the issue, his latest book focuses on specific tactics to develop and maintain a suitable sense of urgency to enable significant change.[12] Of what relevance is this to the church?

First, Kotter rightly names the lack of urgency as the leading reason for lack of movement. Most people experience church as a rather static affair. Church leaders know full well how hard it is to regain momentum once things have settled down. A sense of urgency tends to collapse after relative successes have been achieved.[13] Complacency must surely account for much (not all) of the spiritual and numerical decline we are experiencing at the moment. Complacency, the opposite of urgency, involves being content with the status quo. In the fast-changing world in which we are destined to live out our calling to be the church, this can be disaster. This is especially important given the systematic decline of Christianity throughout the Western world—this is no time for being sinfully smug.

The adventurous church thrives on a sense of holy urgency, and missional movements are built on it. Says Kotter, "If the sense of urgency is not high enough and complacency is not low enough, everything else that we seek to do will become much more difficult."[14] Ironically enough, it is because of our successes that we can so easily slip into complacency. And it doesn't have to be recent success; we have a long tradition of basking in old revivals. Kotter continues, "Urgency leads to success, leads to complacency. At no time are these natural forces stronger than after people have worked very hard and have been rewarded by a visible, unambiguous win."[15] Take for instance the world of sport: in rugby (which both of us love), the time when the team is most vulnerable is immediately after they have scored against their opponents.

According to Kotter, leaders who are successful in creating a missional urgency will utilize the following behaviors:[16]

They create emotionally compelling experiences. When engendering authentic, deeply grounded spiritual urgency, missional leaders should aim for the heart. Intellectual affirmation of ideas is simply not enough, nor are philosophy statements, endless white papers, or mere talk. True urgency involves the heart, engaging people holistically with a passionate and compelling determination to *move, and succeed, now.* "The challenge is to fold a rational case directed toward the mind into an experience that is very much aimed at the heart."[17]

They model urgency in their behavior on an ongoing basis. As is the case in any set of core values, they are better modeled than discussed. Never underestimate the sheer moral power of a person living their philosophy. In the hands of good leadership, it's contagious, and it's the best way to change organizational behaviors. A sense of urgency provides a viable mechanism with which to discern what is necessary and what is not. Keeping this up on a daily basis will model the culture you wish to embed.

They look for the possibilities in crises. A useful crisis creates a situation that cannot be resolved by incremental change. When one is on a "burning platform," the crisis causes one to move, looking for an opportunity. Control systems are important, but don't let damage control eliminate an opportunity to mobilize needed action. A crisis can be used to create urgency and to position an organization for the future. Fear and anger can kill hope. The heart needs hope in order to act with passion, conviction, optimism, and resolve.[18] If external events do not create a crisis, it must fall to leadership to create the appropriate conditions for urgency. However, discernment is needed here. Whatever we create must be associated with *real* missional problems, and not just be a ploy.[19]

They confront naysayers effectively. Naysayers are highly skilled urgency killers, and the church is full of them. They can be powerful barriers to missional engagement and progress. They are not true skeptics, who serve a good purpose by curbing naive enthusiasm and can be convinced by evidence. Rather, naysayers will discredit people and derail the process. They continue to question the information and demand more proof. They disrupt useful conversation and cause delay and frustration. You can't ignore them. You can't co-opt them. You must distract them, push them out of the organization, or expose their behaviors in a socially acceptable way so that social pressure will shut them down.

They keep urgency urgent. Speaking of organizations in general, Kotter says, "With a culture of urgency, people deeply value the capacity to grab new opportunities, avoid new hazards, and continually find ways to win. Behaviors that are the norm include being constantly alert, focusing externally, moving fast, stopping low-value-added activities that absorb time and effort, relentlessly pushing for change when it is needed, and providing the leadership to produce smart change no matter where you are in the hierarchy."[20]

 The ultimate solution to the problem of spiritual complacency is to create a systematically embedded culture of *holy* urgency. This holy urgency is not to be confused with the frenzied activity that tyrannizes and drives so many people and makes them sick; rather, it arises from that sense of holiness that is a necessary prerequisite for godly change. Things are wrong and need to be put right, and the time is now. We are to put our lives in God's hands. Such holy urgency involves the faith of leap, because it recognizes that while we are part of the problem, we are also part of the solution, and we are called to immediate action in our lives and communities. Redemption is seeking to take place in and through us, and we must cooperate with it.

Leading in Liminality

It's commonly understood that an extreme situation can call forth either cowardice or heroism from the very people you would least expect it. There's nothing like a good crisis to reveal the character of the soul or an organization. When one is leading because one's life, and the lives of others, depends on it, then perhaps the best qualities of leadership shine through. This is particularly true when it comes to the issue of leadership and leadership development—strategic areas of focus for the missional church.

Clearly, leading in a life-or-death situation is different from managing in more routine, or even in crisis, circumstances. US Marine Colonel Thomas Kolditz did a unique, long-term study on the nature of leadership in precisely such conditions. In spite of the extreme nature of the research, we believe that his findings on what he calls *in extremis* leaders have clear relevance for those of us who are involved in leading the church through times of massive upheaval and change. His insights are important affirmations as we factor adventure and liminality in the equation of leadership in the church. They include, among others, that

- In extremis leaders are inherently motivated because of the danger of the situations in which they're working; therefore, leaders don't need to use conventional motivational methods or cheerleading.
  . . .
- In extremis leaders embrace continuous learning, typically because they and their followers need to rapidly scan their environments to determine the level of threat and danger they're facing. . . .
- In extremis leaders share the risk their followers face. This isn't just grandstanding; leaders truly share—and even take on greater— risks in in extremis situations. Leaders in other environments

43

should keep this in mind: don't ask your followers to do anything you wouldn't do yourself.

- In extremis leaders share a common lifestyle with their followers. . . . all leaders should consider how much they truly have in common with the rest of their organization. [For instance, the issue of highly unequal pay scales does say something about the nature of leadership.] . . .

- Dangerous situations demand a high level of mutual trust. In extremis leaders trust their team, and they themselves can be trusted. And even if someone's life isn't at stake in an organization, his or her livelihood may be, so do everything you can to be trustworthy and to trust your team to do what [they are chosen] to do.

- High-risk environments demand mutual loyalty between leader and followers. . . . Leaders should do everything they can to foster a culture of mutual loyalty.[21]

Extrapolating from this, we can say that in situations when our lives (or organizations or careers) are at risk, general principles from standard management practice need to be sharpened and their relative degree of importance modified. First, for Kolditz, the most crucial factor for the in extremis leader is to concentrate on the external environment and learn from it what action to take, rather than focus on motivating his/her team.

Alan was watching a documentary on World War II recently. One of the interviewees, Richard Trigaskis, a war correspondent assigned to the front, made this startling comment that highlights how external threat can hone the senses and focus the mind: "There is just something about being in the middle of a battle—alive, yet inches from death. The thought of the danger itself stirs the imagination." As weird as it sounds to those of us more accustomed to a safer form of church leadership, the intensity of an external threat itself energizes those exposed to it. This should sound familiar to leaders who understand fully the external, and oftentimes threatening, mission context around them.

Second, we want to affirm that adventurous leaders must be willing to share with their followers in the risks with which they are confronted, rather than look for cover. Instead of adopting the aloof, hierarchical, top-down approach to leadership, we should, like the biblical leaders (Moses, David, Jesus, Paul), *lead from the front and*

44

not from the rear. The way we said this in Forge Mission Training Network, for instance, is that the teacher must also be a practitioner. We must all have a hand in, and a direct stake in, the ideas we are proclaiming—we must be personally risking and experiencing what we are calling others to do. Our capacity to be inspirational leaders, not simply transactional ones, hinges on this.

This also applies to the degree with which we identify with the life and experience of followers. We cannot be, or even seem to be, motivated by money and personal prestige. Kolditz reminds us, "Leadership is about the success of your people, not about you."[22] He's right: authentic missional leadership emphasizes the development of hope, resilience, and optimism within a highly ethical framework. "To be a leader is not to hold down a position or perform a job: it is to develop a character that is inextricably linked to giving purpose, motivation, and direction to others."[23] Therefore the "impression management" so many church leaders fall prey to, which is intended to make sure that the leader appears to be selfless, concerned, and humble, is doomed to fail. And so is leader development training that focuses solely on knowledge, skills (such as decision making, communication, and planning), and abilities. In liminal situations, character matters supremely. In the church where Jesus is Lord, it is of supreme importance, and it is based squarely on the model of leadership that he provides for us.

This is not to say that skill isn't important; liminal leaders need to be highly competent (and perceived as such) so as to engender the team's trust and loyalty. And the capacity to critically analyze a situation and respond quickly is a fundamental aspect of all leadership. Given the nature of liminal situations, missional leaders need to know how to assess risk and determine when to halt an activity and walk away—and not be afraid to tell the truth about it—and when to continue such activity. The same honest self-critical analysis should also apply when there has been a major performance failure, so as to find and correct systemic weaknesses throughout the organization, not just the initially affected area.[24]

Our own approach to leadership development squares with what can be learned from the in extremis situation. At Forge we took the view that leadership development for a more liminal adventuresome church will go beyond mere theological ideas and ministry skills by

1. emphasizing leader-follower training in live-action contexts;
2. using a primarily inspirational and secondarily informational approach;
3. telling stories of real situations, particularly about what emerging leaders will be facing immediately after graduation;
4. providing peer-to-peer mentoring and sharing of knowledge; and
5. studying not only historical cases but also "live" cases.

The Upside of Down: The By-Products of Liminality

All this talk about adventure, risk, and in extremis leadership sounds pretty exhausting. But these are the necessary elements of liminality—that neither-here-nor-there place to which the church is called. The church can neither retreat to safe institutionalization nor abandon its faith altogether. It is called *out*—out beyond itself into the liminal place of mission. Such a neither-here-nor-there space calls forth a capacity for relentless change. It forces us to be a constantly learning community, with agility and a propensity for risk-taking and movement. And shouldn't anyone related to the Holy God that we worship be in a continual state of change? To know God is to change. Besides, human maturity is predicated on our continued willingness to learn and to grow. But we don't want to give the false impression that change, journey, and liminality always involve death-defying deeds to qualify for a genuine gospel adventure. Acts of love and mercy themselves embody courage and advance the cause of Jesus in our world.

For all the insecurity that an adventurous Christianity-of-the-Road brings, the benefits far outweigh the costs. Conversely, in the nonadventurous, supposedly more secure life, the costs far outweigh the advantages. The loss of pathos, authenticity, and living reality to our faith and experience of Jesus's church is a high price to pay for comfort and convenience. A life lived in fear is a life half lived. Likewise, a church addicted to security and safety is not the church of Jesus Christ; it is in reality something else.

But a sense of urgency can create a honed intelligence and receptivity to change. It seems that this is the case when God's people find themselves on the edges of the norm, in places of liminality, living within an Adventure that is unfolding as they act in it. As the writer of Hebrews pointed out to his predominantly Jewish readership, true faith emerges when people are confronted by liminal experiences, be it Abraham and his journeys, Joseph in jail, Moses and the burning bush, the Exodus events and the associated Sinai revelations, Elijah in the desert, David on the run or at war, the Babylonian captivity, Jesus and his community, the book of Acts, Paul's journeys, Peter's letters to the "exiles," John's banishment on Patmos, and so forth. Revelation downloads and theology is at its densest when we are receptive to God because of conditions of spiritual extremity, urgency, and liminality.

Extreme conditions are nothing new to God's people. Consider Augustine's emotional liminality before God, the sheer daring of the amazing Celtic missionaries, Luther and his reforms, Francis passionately forsaking comfort to be with the poor and his brave mission to the Muslim world, Wesley and his journeys, the monastic mystics in their extreme states, Hudson Taylor pioneering the inland mission in China, Livingston in Africa, the liminal outcasts of the Azusa Street revival that sparked a worldwide movement of 500 million people. These are all situations when people and movements experienced the Holy Spirit in profound, history-altering ways, the fruits of which have added to the inherited wisdom of all God's people.

Following this, we can therefore say on principle that those who, prompted by God and gospel, and following Jesus, push out into the unknown in the holy quest for a better world *will* know God more profoundly than those who stay behind.

The idea of progress is predicated on the assumption that we have not arrived at a state of perfection, that we need to strive toward more faithful ways of being the church. A holy unrest therefore lies at the root of the church's progress. In fact, all renewal originates from the sense that there is more to this than we are currently experiencing; it is a gracious work of the Holy Spirit to awaken us to this need. The people who respond can rightly be called pioneers and saints. Jewish theologian Louis Jacobs puts it this way:

> So it has been throughout the ages. Progress has been possible only because of the heroic efforts of ardent pioneers who dared everything

in obedience to the voice of God. At first they were ridiculed, condemned, and persecuted, while those who benefitted from their self-sacrifice and devotion looked on without making the slightest effort to help. Only after victory had been won, did these others begin to tread with ease the path smoothed for them in anguish and with tears.[25]

Becoming an adventurous, liminal church means getting over risk aversion. Often the difference between a successful person (or organization) and a failure lies not in having better abilities or ideas, but in having the courage to bet on one's ideas, to take a calculated risk—and to act.[26] Risk-ability is vital to learning and innovation.

The Burning Platform

Innovation usually arises out of a sense of need, even desperation, as organizations strive to keep the edge. Living systems theory maintains, rightly, that the sweet spot of innovation takes place on "the edge of chaos," or on what is called "a burning platform"—a situation where the organization is threatened with possible dissolution.

For instance, Donald Kuratko notes that certain environmental factors cause entrepreneurs to emerge. One major factor is *displacement*—political, cultural, economic, and geographical.[27] Being placed into radically new contexts requires an almost total relearning of everything we thought we knew—for example, when one goes to a completely foreign culture. This in turn can trigger the entrepreneurial spirit, because such displacement puts a person and an organization in an environment that creates the possibility of "opportunity recognition." One of the rules of innovation is *Think like a beginner, not an expert*—a precursor to innovation.

When we started Forge Mission Training Network, we recognized the desperate need for entrepreneurial gifting to help us get beyond the current missional impasse in the West. So we developed a philosophy of education that incorporated a lively sense of innovation and entrepreneurship. We didn't have to look far to find a profound way to engender innovation in our interns; in fact, we found it all within the educational philosophy inherent in discipleship itself. For us it meant putting our interns "at risk." If they are standing within their current realm of expertise, then they are only going to learn what they already know, or perhaps even confirm their ignorance. So the learners take one step out of their comfort zone, closer to the edge of chaos, and then another half step so they are "at risk" of real failure. This sets the agenda for the learning journey over the next year. If the liminal situation can be sustained, then real, lasting, paradigm-shifting learning will occur. And hey, Jesus did this exceptionally well with his mob of half-baked disciples.

Inherent in the vocation of discipleship is the call to the kind of extreme liminality that a cross will bring (see Matt. 10:38–39; 16:24–25). In principle, all disciples are meant to integrate this upon their decision to follow Jesus. He warns his disciples of persecution (Matt. 5:11; Luke 21:12; John 12:25) and troubles, but our Lord has overcome it, and so have we in him (John 16:33). Liminality is locked into the equation from the very beginning so that we should not need convincing later on. We are people who have died to our own agenda, we belong to Jesus and his cause (1 Cor. 6:20), we are his servants (Rom. 6:20–22) and ambassadors (2 Cor. 5:20), and we must run for the prize (1 Cor. 9:24) and prepare ourselves for our calling with the discipline of a soldier (2 Tim. 2:3–4). In short, he is the Lord—we are not in control; he is.

This is the fellowship of the King, the people of the cross. The Greek word for witness is *martyrion* and lies at the root of the English word for *martyr*, thus uniting the idea of witness with potential suffering and even death for the person and cause of Jesus. If suffering should come our way (and we would hope it doesn't), we trust that we too would be found faithful. What we know from sisters and brothers who do suffer persecution is that they cling to Jesus and to community in ways we can only dream about. A truth that is suffered for is a personal truth.

It takes a healthy community to endure persecution. In his reflections on friendship and risk, Paul Waddell makes the observation that "it is much easier to take the risk of loving someone when we know we are loved and cherished by another."[28] In other words, the presence of a loving, witnessing community makes it easier to take the risk of extending love to someone outside the community, even when it is dangerous for us to do so. All this leads Scott Bader-Saye to say, "There can be no solution to the problem of fear without the existence of communities capable of bearing fear together."[29]

2

Jesus Is My Disequilibrium

Where Friends Become Comrades

Simply being alone can make us feel vulnerable. Being alone can make it difficult to put danger and fear into perspective. Without the presence of others to balance our perspectives, to strengthen our resolve, and to share our risks, living courageously can feel like a daunting task.

—Scott Bader-Saye

All for one and one for all!
—The Three Musketeers

Humans are inherently social creatures, and as such we learn to be courageous pretty much the way we learn everything else—by being with, observing, and modeling other people. The qualities we need to *be* good are shaped by sharing a life together with other people who help us to become good. As theologian Scott Bader-Saye contends,

Virtues are learned by being with others who embody the virtues. We learn to be virtuous by seeing virtuous people act in virtuous ways. Lacking the community in which the virtues are being sought and lived, one would be hard pressed to develop any of the virtues, including courage.[1]

But the contemporary church, by not being a place of courage and adventure, perpetuates a moral anxiety that fosters an awkwardness toward its wider community. Many church folk, in their self-conscious attempt to be overtly morally upright, emit all the wrong signals, thus messing with people's perception of the gospel. Says Alison Morgan in *The Wild Gospel*:

> Anxiety . . . means that insofar as we do engage with the world out there, our contribution is mostly a worried attempt to restrain it; afraid for our children, we strive to uphold the moral standards of a sliding culture by campaigning against abortion or disapproving of stories about wizards. The result is that we keep our moral and spiritual integrity, but our witness is lost.[2]

Such timidity and anxiety leaves the church as a retreatist, frightened, ineffective organization. Morgan goes on: "We have set up private clubs for those whose leisure interest is religion."[3] Church folk settle into patterns of institutional life that turn the focus inward, and become content with self-preservation. When churches displace mission for maintenance, they become unlikely places for individuals to develop a more adventurous form of discipleship, "since the temptation to self-preservation so quickly shuts down any courageous action."[4]

This is why we must learn from great missional movements—especially the ones that suffered for their cause—because "they embodied the most powerful witness to courage we can imagine," as Bader-Saye puts it.

> [The martyrs] recognized that discipleship would require risk, but they did not step back from it. They lived for something bigger than self-preservation, so the threat of death could not scare them into unfaithfulness. They were sustained by communities that not only taught them courage, but promised to tell their stories to future generations,

assuring them that their sacrifice would not be forgotten. The courage
of the martyr relies upon the courage of the community that dares
to keep the martyr's story alive. Today more than ever, our churches
need to be telling and celebrating their stories.[5]

Communit-eh?

We were always meant to venture out, but we were never meant to do
it alone. When Jesus kicked off the mission that we are continuing
now, he didn't commission rugged, individualistic swashbucklers
haphazardly forging their own destinies in life, but rather he initiated
a *movement* destined to be the community of the faithful who are in
the end found worthy to worship before the throne (Rev. 21). It is a
widely recognized fact that Westerners tend to distort Jesus's intent
by reading the Bible as written to, and about, individuals. Not so.
The Bible is written to *communities*, be it Israel or the church, and
it is written to foster community, whether it be the national identity
of Israel or the faith community of the church. Just as there is no
such thing as an Israel-less Jew, there is no such thing as a churchless
Christian (1 Cor. 12:13). Our very identity as God's people is bound
up in the collective identity of being an *ecclesia*—a group of people
called, named, redeemed, ruled, and loved by Jesus (Rom. 1:1–3;
Eph. 4; Col. 1:1–3; 1 Peter 2:9–10; Rev. 1–3). We are never going to
be the church that Jesus built if we do not take community seriously.

In *The Forgotten Ways* Alan suggests that missional movements
that actually transform their world comprise a dynamic network of
communities that overcome their innate human instinct to "huddle
and cuddle" and form themselves around a common mission that
calls them onto a dangerous journey to unknown places. Movements
happen when the church manages to shake off its collective fears and
plunges into the mission of God in the world, where, while experiencing liminality and disorientation, they also get to encounter God
and each other in a new way. Similarly, in *Exiles*, Michael explores
the relationship of discipleship and community in calling us to live
as exiles—followers of Jesus who operate from the margins of culture and, because of liminal circumstance, are recovering a much
more biblical form of community. Either way, we were trying to
describe the kind of community that is able to integrate adventure

53

Communitas — liminality

Communitas == communal
phenomena formed in adventurous
mission

and movement, a community that experiences a *togetherness* that happens only among people inspired by the vision of a better world and attempting to do something about it. The name we gave to the communal phenomenon that forms in adventurous mission and liminal discipleship is *communitas*.[6]

Allow us to briefly reintroduce the term here. The best way to think about it is to imagine the kind of band of companions that form in the context of adventure, around a common ordeal, a challenge, a task, or in pursuit of a mission. This entry into a verge-like experience is called *liminality*. Liminality, remember, involves adventure, risk, journey, engagement, and courage and was explored as the subject of the previous chapter. When liminality "happens" (it can be deliberately cultivated), it fundamentally restructures the nature of preexisting relationships, friendships emerge from mere associations, and *comradeship* evolves from preexisting friendships. Being immersed in a communitas, participants experience an almost mystical *togetherness* that occurs only among a group of people engaging in a task bigger than itself. A different genre of love emerges from the experience of communitas—one that cannot emerge in the more static form of associations. The bonding is deep; people get to *need* each other, they get to know and rely on each other. They have to (sometimes for sheer survival), to overcome the liminal challenge in whatever form it is experienced.

Keep in mind that there is a direct and indissoluble link between liminality and communitas; they are two sides of the same coin. Unfortunately, we can't have the one without the other. Therefore we will often join the two terms (liminality-communitas) to ensure that we appreciate the necessary dialectic inherent between the two aspects.

We cannot shake the impression that the church Jesus built was meant to experience this form of togetherness . . . and lots of it. And not just for the sake of love and fellowship, but because we have a mission that requires it! Mission propels us out of self-concern to other-concern, from holy huddle to venturing out into God's world. And mission, encapsulating as it does the purpose of the church, has always been vital to the equation of ecclesia that Jesus intended in the first place—it goes to the reason of why we exist at all! Much more is gathered up in this topic than we might first imagine.

Dr. Turner, I Presume . . .

We have adopted the terms *liminality* and *communitas* from the seminal writings of Victor Turner, an anthropologist who spent much of his life studying the various rites of passage among African people groups, particularly the Ndembu of southern Africa.[7] He used the term *liminality* to describe a transition process accompanying a fundamental change of state or social position. He particularly focused on the initiation ceremonies where boys are transitioned into being men. These situations of liminality constitute a kind of test about whether the participants will be allowed to return to society and to transition to the next level in the prevailing social structure.

Cast out of the village and made to live in the jungle, fending for themselves and being visited regularly by the community holy men to be taught the lore and learning of adulthood, the initiates find themselves on this threshold. Liminality therefore applies to that situation where people find themselves in an in-between, marginal state in relation to the surrounding society, a place that could involve significant marginalization, ordeal, disorientation, and sometimes danger.

For example, in some tribes, younger boys are kept under the care of the women until initiation age—around thirteen. At the appropriate time, the men sneak into the female compound of the village at night and "kidnap" the lads. The boys are blindfolded, roughed up, and herded out of the village into the bush. They are circumcised, then left to fend for themselves in the wild African bush for up to six months. They are in a threshold experience. Once a month the elders of the tribe go to meet them to help debrief and mentor them. But on the whole they have to find both inner and outer resources to cope with the ordeal without any outside assistance.

During this time, the initiates move from being disoriented and individualistic to developing a deep bond of comradeship forged in the testing conditions of liminality. Turner observed that during the period of liminality, the initiates progressively achieve a release from conformity to general norms and experience a profound and collective sentiment for each other—a "super community," a transforming experience of connection with oneself, with others, and with the universe. Thought by Turner to most approximate a religious experience, he called this wonderful experience of interconnectedness between initiates *communitas*. Communitas in his view happens in situations where individuals are driven to find each other through a common experience of ordeal, humbling, transition, and marginalization. It involves intense feelings of social togetherness and belonging brought about by having to rely on each other in order to survive. If the boys emerge from these experiences, they are reintroduced into the tribe as men. They are thus accorded the full status of manhood—they are no longer considered boys. The process looks something like this:

Figure 2.1

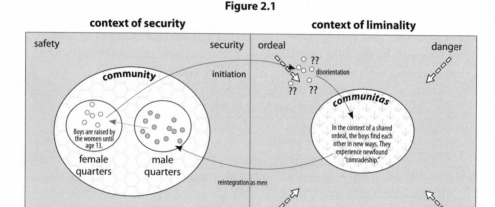

We were recently given a marvelous illustration of the liminality-communitas in the blockbuster movie *Avatar*, where the story's protagonist, Jake Sully, with the guidance of his sponsor, Neytiri, and under the harsh tutelage of the established warriors, is initiated into the adult Na'vi culture. Through the process, he is not only initiated into the people's life philosophy and story, he is called to embark (with the other young initiates) on a sometimes death-defying process of learning to be a true warrior worthy of the people. The movie, like many of its type, is mythic in structure and simply draws on the use of collective memories and on what we already know about how societies transfer cultural vigor and identity through rituals of liminality-communitas.

Far from being damaging to social structures, regular experiences of communitas strengthen a society. While societies need the stability of normal life, they also need the liminal experience of communitas. This is what pushes society forward, infusing it with a freshness and vitality that comes from the deeper communion created by the threshold experience. It is the almost mystical sense of comradeship experienced in communitas that sows the seeds of cultural regeneration back in normal society. These bonds deepen relationships and enrich the community for life.

Turner went so far as to detach the phenomena of liminality and communitas from rites of passage; he suggested that it is possible for societies to experience them regularly, not just at early adulthood. The social modes of normal society (structure) and communitas (what he calls *anti-structure*) can and do exist simultaneously in a society, and no society can function adequately without this dialectic.[8] In fact, the loss of meaningful rituals of initiation into adulthood is considered by some to be the main cause of delinquency and malformed adult identity, particularly amongst men, in the West.[9] This at least partly explains young urban kids' desire to join the many gangs populating the inner cities. Turner dared to suggest that in the dialectic between communitas and normal society lies the hope for the future of that society.

> People or societies in a liminal phase are a kind of institutional capsule or pocket which contains the germ of future social developments, of societal change.[10]

This is so different from what we have usually identified as *community*, particularly the way the church has used this term. So-called Christian community is often portrayed as an inwardly focused gathering of people, committed to worshiping God together, to regular attendance at Sunday worship and small groups, to Bible study, and to encouraging and building each other up. There is very little that can be called liminal in the average American churchgoer's experience of Christianity. Certainly churches should be "safe places" where members can be open and vulnerable together, receive support, understanding, and pastoral care. We have no objection to these things, but perhaps that it is only part of the story, and they have become ends in themselves. The safety-obsessed church lacks the inner dynamic to foster profound missional impact in our time. But thankfully all the potential for real communitas lies dormant in them. All it takes is a little adventure to activate it in order for them to once again become the revolutionary movement that God intended for the world.

Communion, Up in the Air

In their research into the nature of high-risk leisure activities, Richard Celsi, Randall Rose, and Thomas Leigh examined the experience of a number of skydiving clubs in the United States. They found that skydivers experienced a kind of communal bliss, or communitas, just as Victor Turner described it. But more than that, skydiving clubs, due to the high-risk nature of their shared activity, were bonded in an extreme fashion. In other words, jumping is the "mission," and it catalyzes an intense bond between fellow jumpers. It is quite literally a collective faith of leap.

Celsi, Rose, and Leigh were able to separate out a number of aspects to the communitas experienced by skydivers. They say that their subjects experienced (1) "flow"—an individual heightened experience; (2) communitas—transcendent group camaraderie; and (3) what they call "phatic communion"—a special form of communication between participants. So perhaps by struggling with even more new and strange terminology, we believe that the bond skydivers experience together can help deepen our understanding of Christian communitas.

The authors found that their subjects described the skydiving act as one of total absorption that provides them with not only thrill and excitement, but also a sense of involvement that transcends mundane experience. In the midst of this complete absorption, they were in the "flow" and nothing else mattered. Celsi et al. take up the point:

> This transcendent state, or "flow experience" . . . occurs when a situation demands total participation from the individual. As such, flow is a phenomenological state where self, self-awareness, behavior, and context form a unitized singular experience. Thus, flow is a state of

total involvement where one moment "flows" holistically into the next without "conscious intervention."[11]

They quote sociologist Mihaly Csikszentmihalyi, who first coined the term *flow*, and who believed the flow experience is the manifestation of a person's true self, unconstrained temporally by convention or by self-awareness.[12] In other words, flow provides a sense of self and self-efficacy that is highly satisfying and self-fulfilling. But flow could be experienced in any activity that requires high levels of concentration. Novelists report being "in the flow" as they write, as do musicians when they play. Celsi et al. discovered that when groups perform an activity that requires total absorption, this sense of flow arises in individuals, but it sets off a number of other responses, primarily communitas. This bond transcends everyday statuses and social roles, as Celsi et al. found among skydivers. They quote one of their subjects as saying,

> Jumpers have a special kind of bond. You have your doctors, professors, lawyers, but you also have your truck drivers, bricklayers, and masons. Out here on the weekends none of that is a factor. What people do and how much money they make just doesn't matter. There's just this closeness here.[13]

In keeping with Turner's finding that liminality is the ordeal that catalyzes communitas, jumpers experience skydiving as a truly liminal state. Celsi et al. put it this way: "Each skydive itself, in microcosm, can be seen as a liminal state between two environmental statuses—physical contact with the earth, plane, or parachute versus free-fall. In this sense, a liminal experience is replicable to all skydivers with each jump."[14]

From flow to shared flow, these skydivers then experience what has been termed a *phatic communion*. Coined by anthropologist Bronislaw Malinowski, phatic communion refers to the special communication that occurs within cultural groups. This is the kind of "insider knowledge"—that *knowing*—that members of a sporting team seem to have with each other, where one player has a seemingly transcendent sense of where another player is going and what he or she is going to do next. The high-risk subculture of skydiving has the

[handwritten marginal notes: "phatic communion = insider knowledge special communication w/in shared groups" and "Special language"]

same mystical connection, a special communication that anticipates behavior as well as communicating shared experience and technical language. It is a special language that joins together members of the cultural community and is little understood by nonmembers. Indeed, comprehension of this special language is held in high esteem as a sign of cultural membership. It is more than the jargon or "in-words" used by some groups to exclude others. It is essential communication required by members to fulfill their contribution to the shared ritualistic experience, whether skydiving, playing football, or undertaking a missional adventure.

In Edward Zwick's powerful World War II film *Defiance*, we meet three Jewish brothers who are forced into hiding from the occupying Nazis in a nearby Belorussian forest. There they discover more Jews, also hiding, and band together to create a makeshift forest community with the hope of outlasting the war. As stories of this renegade community filter throughout the region, more refugees from Nazi oppression join them, and over time the brothers realize they need a more sophisticated approach to the collection of food and the building of shelter in order to survive the harsh Russian winter that looms. The small ragged band of refugees develops into a well-organized society, sheltering deep within the isolated Lipiczanska forest.

Director and screenwriter Zwick makes a point of not showing any of the war that rages on around the forest, keeping his camera firmly focused on the refugee community. He portrays the minutia of their society: wood collection, food preparation, the posting of sentries. Babies are born. Couples fall in love and are married. A rabbi conducts worship. The passage of time is discernible only by the changing seasons. This almost claustrophobic approach to storytelling helps to establish the intense level of relationship experienced by the characters, because even though some semblance of society is developed, we know that the forest community is a community under extreme pressure. Beyond the forest, the German forces begin to close the net on them.

Defiance was not a popular film, and the critics seemed perturbed by its length (137 minutes), the bleakness of the story, and its visual drabness (set almost entirely in a dark, snow-covered forest). But these are essential elements in the retelling of the Bielski brothers' story. The unremittingly miserable conditions at Lipiczanska, the long tense hours of not knowing when the Nazis will attack, punctuated occasionally by bursts of violence and bloodshed, aren't exactly the stuff of Hollywood blockbusters. But *Defiance* is a sensational depiction of communitas. Despite their differences, which are not inconsiderable, the three brothers—Tuvian, Zus, and Asael—are united by a common foe and a common mission. The forest society they fashion isn't without internal conflict, but such conflict is dwarfed by the challenges they face together. These challenges—surviving winter, evading Nazis, foraging for food—form the basis of their mission, and it is this mission that shapes and sustains their community.

The same spirit experienced by skydivers—flow, communitas, phatic communion—is also evident in *Defiance*. And while skydivers create an artificial ordeal, the Bielskis had theirs thrust upon them. We acknowledge that these are dramatic examples of societies forged by the liminal experience of danger. But we suggest that it is possible for Christians to enter the liminality of mission and experience the same catalyzing effects on their sense of community.

Liminality-Communitas by the Book

But liminality-communitas is not merely the scholarly concern of academic anthropologists and skydiving theorists. It is not only a common human experience but turns out to be a thoroughly biblical one, the recovery of which is vital to fostering a genuinely missional ecclesiology. In fact, when we examine Scripture with the liminality-communitas framework in mind, we cannot avoid the conclusion that the *most theologically fertile sections* are formed in times of *precisely* such situations.

As we have seen in chapter 1, the main clusters of revelation seem to come in times of extremity. And when we consider the biblical stories that have inspired the people of God throughout the ages, we find that they are stories involving adventures of the spirit in the context of challenge. In fact, that is *exactly why* they inspire.

Actors in the Story

Take Abram (later Abraham), for instance, who with his entire extended family (estimated to be about seventy people and their belongings) is called by an invisible God to leave house and home and all that is familiar to undertake a very risky journey to a land that at that stage remained a mere promise by this God. And when we look at the various experiences they have along the way, stories that have shaped all subsequent faith (e.g., the offering of Isaac), they are not safe little bedtime stories. Rather they call us to a dangerous form of faithfulness that echoes the faithfulness of Abraham (Gal. 3:15ff; Heb. 11:8–13). Or when we explore the profoundly liminal Exodus experience, we find that this very tricky journey indelibly shaped the people of God and continues to do so to this very day. It was also the context of the substantial revelation of God in his covenant with his people. The same can be said of the exile into Babylon many centuries later—this was an extreme situation that changed the whole way Israel related to her God, and still does. The prophets spoke the Word of God into such contexts of extremity. And it was precisely when the people of God settled down and "forgot YHWH" (see Deut. 4:23–31) that they had to be spiritually disturbed once again by the prophets. To awaken the people to their lost calling, the prophets recalled the dangerous memories about fires on the mountain and pursuing armies and a God who lovingly redeems a people and enters into a sacred and eternal covenant with them. This sounds pretty liminal to me.

As we consider the lives and ministries of Samuel, Elijah, Samson, and David and his band, and ask what conditions they encountered, we come up with the consistent themes of liminality and communitas. And when we come to the New Testament, we need to look only to the life of Jesus, who had nowhere to rest or lay his head, and who discipled his followers *on the road* in the real, dangerous conditions of an occupied land and against a hostile and dodgy religious elite. So much so that discipleship à la Jesus looks awfully like those risky initiation rites that the African kids have to go through. It was both costly ("deny yourself and follow me") and dangerous ("if they hated me, they will hate you too"), but that came with the territory of discipleship.

To find these themes in abundance, look at the life of Paul. He describes it vividly for us in 2 Corinthians. Whippings, beatings, imprisonment, and shipwrecks can hardly be called "safe, secure, comfortable, and convenient." Yet through these experiences, he and his apostolic band totally realign the course of history around the gospel of Jesus Christ. The book of Acts is so brimful with liminality-communitas that it reads like a rollicking adventure story.

Communitas describes well the sense of companionship that the disciples must have felt. With Jesus leading the charge, they experienced a liminality and communitas so exquisite that it eventually altered the history of the world forever. While we sometimes mistakenly imagine the company of Christ to be a happy band of vagabonds traveling carefree around Judea, we need to remember that the Twelve, in particular, had left everything to follow Jesus. They were like the African initiates. They had separated themselves from the mainstream of their society at great personal cost. They are a perfect example of a liminal society that lies at the heart of defining our own Story.

Strangers and Aliens

A particularly poignant way to conceive of ourselves as a communitas is to recover the biblical teaching that incorporates images of exile and pilgrimage. While the theme winds its way through all of Scripture, the book of Hebrews is the book par excellence for calling us to be an ongoing communitas . . . or in the words of the writer, to be God's pilgrim people who will faithfully testify, by their continuing status as exiles and strangers, to their desire for a better country, a heavenly city, a homeland (Heb. 11). By their very pilgrimage, they give witness that they are in fact already citizens of that community. Hebrews pictures the Christian community on earth as living like Abraham in tents "in the land of promise, as in a foreign land" (Heb. 11:9 RSV). The noted ecclesiologist Paul Minear asserts that "the church is by its very nature composed of tent dwellers."[15]

In fact, all the books in the last third of the New Testament focus on the church as a pilgrim people. From Hebrews to Revelation we have a variation of this theme from different perspectives.[16] New Testament scholar Scott Nash points us to a helpful illustration of this in the subtitle of John Bunyan's classic *The Pilgrim's Progress*. The extended title of the book, typical to nineteenth-century publishing, was unbelievably long . . . [taking big breath] it says:

The Pilgrim's Progress from This World to That Which Is to Come, Delivered under the Similitude of a Dream, Wherein Is Discovered the Manner of His Setting Out, His Dangerous Journey, and Safe Arrival in the Desired Country. The last part of his title suggests three dimensions of the pilgrim life useful for us to consider:

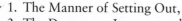

1. The Manner of Setting Out,
2. The Dangerous Journey, and
3. The Safe Arrival in the Desired Country.

We have, then, a beginning, a middle, and an end to the adventure of pilgrimage.[17]

Significantly, these three dimensions of pilgrimage square well with the theme of the last nine books of the New Testament:

The book of Hebrews, which appears first in this group, focuses on the beginning of the journey. While Hebrews deals with many subjects, its central theme is a call to lifelong pilgrimage and courage to continue in spite of the odds. The books of James, 1 Peter, 2 Peter, 1 John, 2 John, 3 John, and Jude all focus on the middle part, the journey itself and warnings about the dangers of being sidelined or getting off track. The last book in this group, Revelation, focuses on the end. It gives a grand vision of the final destination and offers encouragement for safe arrival in the desired country.[18]

Another aspect about the pilgrim imagery is worth mentioning: God's chosen people are destined to be like spiritual vagabonds, refugees and exiles, and as such they are not able (or allowed) to blend in with the locals. They are different, they are strangers that exist in that limbo of exile where, as we have seen, authentic life transitions are accomplished. It is no accident that the Bible insists that believers identify with the poor, the mistreated, and the prisoners (e.g., Heb. 10:32–34; 13:2–3).

Taken together, these books and others (e.g., the Pentateuch, the Prophets, the Gospels, and Acts) teach us that the journey we are called to take is

beset with difficulties. Fear and inertia may endanger the beginning. Pitfalls may lie along the trail threatening the journey itself. Some pitfalls may come from without in terms of wrong turns or dangerous terrain. Some pitfalls may come from within in terms of disagreement about directions or dissension among the travelers themselves. Even near the end, pilgrims may lose sight of the final destination or may despair of ever reaching it. Journeys worth making are seldom easy.[19]

The Rhythm of Life

It turns out the concept of communitas isn't as unusual as it first appears. It is not just embedded in our deepest theology, it is structured into the very rhythm of life itself. So, if it does appear odd to us, this is likely because we have somehow managed to remove ourselves from the challenging spiritual discipline found in liminality-communitas.

Surely we can recall periods of our lives when this was true. Think of any group of people in a liminal state, and in all likelihood they will have experienced a deeper sense of community than those who have opted for a safe experience. From the New Yorkers' experience of 9/11 to the deadlines at work, from surviving and reconstructing after a national disaster to playing in a sports game final, liminality-communitas is everywhere present. Heck, at the end of a weekend church camp, everyone has bonded and cries when it's time to leave. If you have ever been on a short-term mission trip overseas, you have felt that special, intimate, profound sense of connection with your fellow travelers. People who experience a war together report that those who didn't simply cannot know the comradeship people in extreme situations experience. Ever wondered why people join gangs? And why they will die for their "homies"? Communitas.

When building houses in Mexico or working in orphanages in Haiti, we connect with others at an entirely different level from that experienced each week in our local church. This isn't just because of the exotic location or the spicy food. It's because we are in a liminal state. We are not living at home, nor are we really living in Mexico. We are in transition, a resident in neither place, really. This sense of liminality, fueled by the challenge of completing certain set tasks, fosters communitas. Even if we find ourselves on a team with people we don't particularly like or whose company we don't much enjoy, the experience of liminality eventually sweeps away our petty differences, bonding us strongly, because we are forced to rely on each other for survival.

It's disturbing to hear young people, recently returned from an experience of liminality and communitas, complain that their church not only doesn't understand their experience, but provides no forums for them to talk about it. As noted earlier, Turner said that those who've tasted communitas are like a capsule that contains the germ of future development and change. We must learn to maximize on the renewal being offered by those who return from liminal journeys.

All for One and One for All

Many people undergo something of a communitas experience in their daily lives. Sporting teams, theatre companies, orchestras, bands, dance troupes—these kinds of societies all know something, perhaps just a whiff, of the experience of communitas. When a group of musicians or dancers are performing, every member must play their part well—not just individually, but in concert with the others. This sense of interdependence can be very exciting. Jazz musicians will speak of the almost spiritual communion they sense when all members of the band are playing in perfect harmony. Any member of a sports team can recall something of the profound sense of intimacy they feel with their teammates, when each of their contributions to the game create a force greater than the sum of their individual parts.

When an amateur theatre group begins rehearsals, it can be just a ragtag assembly of would-be thespians. But when onstage, galvanized by the threat of the impending opening night, they are transformed into something else. With the script as their guide, they are forced together by the "ordeal" of knowing they will soon be giving public performances. One young amateur actor once told one of us that he felt a greater sense of belonging and acceptance in his theatre company than in his church. We suppose he thought it had to do with the quality of the people in the theatre as compared with those in the church. But the fact remains that churches are full of marvelous, kind, caring people, every bit as accepting as theatre people. The fundamental difference is that churches are working on community, while an amateur theatre group is forming a kind of communitas.

Turner himself was onto this phenomenon. Later in his career he began to apply his theories to American subcultures like artists. In his essay *Liminality and Communitas*, he notes,

Prophets and artists tend to be liminal and marginal people, "edge-men," who strive with a passionate sincerity to rid themselves of the clichés associated with status incumbency and role-playing and to enter into vital relations with other men in fact or imagination.[20]

He believed that artists, including actors, musicians, dancers, painters, and the like, were the very people most capable of propelling society forward, because they had stepped into a liminal state and had experienced a communitas unlike anything possible in normal society. If you've spent any time with artists of any kind, you'll know what he means. When artists meet for the first time, they share the knowing smile of someone who has stepped out of the respectability of mainstream suburban life. Their shared liminality opens them up immediately to each other—although strangers, they are family.

Putting It All on the Line

This is no different from men and women who have served together in the armed forces, particularly those who saw combat together. On Veterans Day we see them gathering for their street marches, nodding with an unspoken respect to each other. They have known a liminality unlike anything the rest of us can imagine. They were separated from mainstream society, sent to a foreign land to undergo a life-and-death ordeal, and then returned to us as different people. Those of us who have known nothing but civilian life can never fully appreciate their experience. It is to each other, to the communitas, that they must turn for real understanding.

This kind of battlefield camaraderie was described by the French knight Jean de Brueil in 1465:

Battle is a joyous thing. We love each other so much in battle. If we see that our cause is just and our kinsmen fight boldly, tears come to our eyes. A sweet joy rises in our hearts, in the feeling of our honest loyalty to each other; and seeing our friend so bravely exposing his body to danger in order to fulfill the commandment of our Creator, we resolve to go forward and die or live with him on account of love. This brings such delight that anyone who has not felt it cannot say how wonderful it is. Do you think someone who feels this is afraid of death? Not in the least! He is so strengthened,

67

so delighted, that he does not know where he is. Truly, he fears nothing in the world.[21]

Some might be squeamish about what seems like the glorification of war, but we don't mean in any way to be lionizing the horrors of mortal combat. We are reminded by the horror of war, though, about the powerful connection that people develop when faced with awesome odds. It's the same connection that explorers like Shackleton or Peary or Lewis and Clark felt with their men. The sense of communitas that Shackleton developed with his crew was legendary. He pledged them his life that he would not let one of them die, and when his *Endurance* expedition got into so much trouble, he traveled thousands of miles in an open boat and then traversed a mountainous island to get help for them, as they waited out a dreadful winter in an upturned rowboat. In return his crew loved him beyond words.

Communitas is not an exclusively male experience by any means. In Cambodia, for instance, it is women who lead many of the effective trade unions, fighting for better work conditions for their colleagues. It is women's groups that fight and lobby the government against the epidemic of domestic violence. A women's media center has been established to raise awareness of the unacceptable levels of rape that beset Cambodian families. During the recent national election, thousands of women were marshaled as independent observers at polling stations to scrutinize the vote-counting process. In Argentina in the 1970s, a group of white-scarved mothers assembled every week in Buenos Aires's main square, under the glare of soldiers of the monstrous military dictatorship of General Videla, to display pictures of their missing children. Their children were numbered among the 30,000 *desaparecido*—literally, the disappeared—of that regime. Called the Madres de la Plaza de Mayo, these mothers banded together to remain the only people in the world to hold Videla's henchmen accountable.

It's the same connection that the suffragette Emmeline Pankhurst and her fiery daughters, Christabel and Sylvia, developed with their "troops" who fought against a society that wouldn't grant women the vote. When one of their number, Emily Wilding Davison, threw herself under the king's horse, Anmer, as it rounded Tattenham Corner in the 1913 English Derby, male society was shocked by the lengths to which these women would go. For the suffragettes, though, the movement was a war, and the communitas that developed was every bit as great as that between male combatants during military campaigns.

Similar groups have developed in Northern Ireland where both Catholic and Protestant mothers of murdered children have been at the forefront of peace and reconciliation movements. In the 1970s Betty Williams and Mairead Corrigan, two bereaved Irish mothers, still grieving for the murders of their own sons and fed up with watching their friends' sons and their nephews die on the streets, formed the Community of Peace People. Initially a women's movement, it said "Enough!" to the never-ending cycle of violence and vengeance that gripped Northern Ireland. Ignored by the male-dominated political parties, the Peace People captured the hearts of thousands of ordinary Irish parents. When Williams and Corrigan were awarded the Nobel Peace Prize for their peace-building work in 1976, Irish politicians were forced to take them seriously.

Thrown together by their liminal state, forced to work against cultural forces massed against them, women's groups around the world know the same kind of communitas that the thirteenth-century French knight Jean de Brueil spoke of earlier. Such communitas is hardened by battle, softened by true and genuine partnership, and forged by a shared vision for a better world.

Everyday Adventure

Some of these stories describe highly intense and extremely risky activities. Are we suggesting that Christian communities could live permanently in this heightened state of awareness? Of course not. But we do think that Christian communities could develop so robust a commitment to serving others that it catalyzes a kind of phatic communion, albeit an everyday version. For a winsome, somewhat more down-to-earth example of this, we turn to an eccentric band of missionaries called the Winking Circle.

In Uxbridge, Ontario, you'll find the most extraordinary communitas, committed to embracing what they call the everyday adventure. Watching their town become slowly absorbed by subdivisions of commuters, chain stores, and big box outlets, this group of friends rallied together to resist the prevailing apathy and launch a mini-revolution. Calling themselves the Winking Circle, they began as one family and a group of local kids who took over a condemned house and began a series of eccentric projects that marked them out against the rest of society.

They started by customizing a bunch of old bikes, welding them into the strangest flotilla of hand-painted choppers, tall bikes (up to five levels high), tireless bikes, low bikes, and all sorts of rolling art machines. Once they started cruising the streets of their sleepy little town on their moving bike sculptures, a spark was ignited and a communitas was forged. The Winking Circle had started a fire of eccentric self-expression, a holdout against the conformity and mind-numbing ordinariness of the lives of those around them. Soon others joined them in their everyday adventure.

When asked what they were doing, they replied that they had turned off their television sets and were starring in their own lives. And the weird bike project was only the beginning. They started to travel to a nearby city to take part in mass bike rides to alert others to their marvelous mission to eccentrify the world. They started bands, designed their own clothes, and screen-printed their T-shirts. They organized shows in halls, basements, and bedrooms. They invented ridiculous hairstyles and strange dance moves. BMX trails were dug in the woods near their town. They built bike and skate ramps and eventually worked with the local township to raise the money and construct their dream ramp—the "Tsunami ramp"—for all to enjoy.

And all along, they filmed all this eccentric activity with handicams to record the insanity for posterity. Eventually, a documentary filmmaker labored over the hundreds of hours of footage to create a video zine, *The Winking Circle*, an audiovisual celebration of everything the group stands for. Of this film, it is claimed,

> Everyone who sees it is impacted in their own way. Kids have been known to shut off the television immediately after watching it to draw or build bike jumps. Jaded television executives are moved to tears, people make their own Winking Circle T-shirts. It has been a springboard for people to remember old dreams and envision new

ones. Numerous people have said that it permanently affected them and the way they think about their place in the world.[22]

All this activity is undergirded and sustained by what the Winking Circle calls "the wisdom of the 3 Beans." It forms the foundation of their community. In the documentary film, they describe the 3 Beans as follows:

> *Create everywhere*: We are creative, not spectators. We personally customize ourselves and our surroundings.
> *Be a fool*: We will not conform. We're not cool. We make up dance moves and try crazy stunts.
> *Redeem everything*: Whether it's a bad situation or a beat-up bicycle, we transform it into something spectacular.

Year after year, more and more young people have joined this community of eccentricity, making it a heroic, energetic, and inclusive underground youth movement. But it hasn't all been smooth sailing for the Winking Circle. Like any good communitas, they have found that when you stand against conformity, apathy, and consumerism, the world fights back. Their first ramps were burnt to the ground by local vandals, and the replacements were continually attacked. Their dream ramp (the fabled Tsunami ramp) was, without any warning, sawn in half and secreted out of town. A national Canadian television program ran a short film produced by the Winking Circle, and took all the credit for it after the film won international awards. And most famously, a global beverage corporation allegedly ripped off the design of their video for one of their marketing campaigns.

Furthermore, trying to sustain the wisdom of the 3 Beans among young people hasn't been easy. As some of them grew older, the daily onslaught of consumer culture began to numb them into apathy. But overall, the effect has been positive. Many Winkers (as they call themselves) have become talented musicians and songwriters. A few bands have been formed, received recording contracts, and gone on tour. Two separate charities have been created: one selling handmade clothing and art to raise money for the poor; another collecting and repairing used bikes to send to Africa. A number of the Winkers have gone on mission trips all over the world to serve those in need. Artistic self-expression remains important for many of those involved. Art cars have been painted and driven. A few entrepreneurial spirits have started their own business. People are going on to study for careers in international development, art therapy, medicine, theatre, graphic design, and the music industry. As they say of themselves, they have been "ruined for the ordinary."

The Winking Circle of Uxbridge, Ontario, is a perfect example of a communitas, a collective of people who find meaningful life together as a result of their shared mission.

Embedding an Adventure Spirituality

How

If we are going to make the change from community to communitas, and not just end up with an unsustainable adrenaline-junkie culture, we must have a sophisticated process to form people into adventurer-disciples. In what follows, we have tried to be guided by what we know from the social sciences, theology, liturgiology, and to be honest, a good dose of educated guesswork. We suggest three points for inculcating an adventurous spirituality: embedding risk and adventure into the culture, developing a new hero system, and ritualizing it into the community.

1. Embed Adventure into the Culture

If we want to become an adventuring church, then liminality-communitas must become part of the very culture of the church/organization. Here are some suggestions about how to do this:

Take risks: Wise risk-taking and courageous actions should be encouraged and ongoing. The organization should value experimentation, engage in church planting as often as possible, and get involved in missional activity that takes its members to the edges of what is comfortable or normal.

Form disciples in community: While we appreciate individual effort and achievement, we need to foster the understanding that we are in this together. Private discovery of meaning is not enough. Meaning is discovered in community—it is a "tribe thing." Beware of the naturally competitive nature of

Westerners here: it should involve movement into space where ongoing transformation can continue, not competitive space where I must continue to define and prove myself. Remember, it is about becoming mature disciples of Jesus and not defining ourselves *over against* others.

Create positive and redemptive experiences: Whatever events and processes we might use to cultivate liminality-communitas, they must involve initiation into something really transformational, good, and positive. Whatever ideas are transferred during liminality-communitas events, they should be saturated with the redeeming power of the gospel of Jesus and not an ideology against, in fear of, angry at, or needing to win over anybody else.

Start young and expect a lifelong journey: Churches are especially advised to develop some form of ritual initiation process whereby children are initiated into the wise risk-taking that forms an essential part of mature discipleship. And don't allow the adults, families, and older folk to think that adventure and risk is a thing of youth. That big cop-out must be avoided at all costs.

Create opportunity to adventure: There need to be regular opportunities and events that people can get involved with. It cannot just be a once-a-year weekend high. It must somehow be structured into Christian life itself.

Do something together: Adventure spirituality must therefore be action-based. Action should be at the heart of the culture. It cannot simply be reduced to a mental process of assimilating theology or the academic study of ethics. This requires the deliberate cultivation of, and rewarding of, courageous action in the life of the community. Everyone should be somehow, and sometimes, involved in adventuring out.

Cultivate genuine spiritual-moral authority: You cannot lead where you will not go; you cannot teach what you do not know. You can only transfer what you already have. If the leaders have not gone through significant liminality-communitas experiences themselves, they really have nothing to say to those they lead. Leaders must lead by example. If not, any attempt by them to develop the culture of adventure and a hero system that incorporates liminality-communitas will result in mere parody and strained symbolization. And while certain events might still be appreciated, it will not fundamentally change the culture.

Tell lots of stories: Tell stories of liminality-communitas and create ample opportunities for others to tell theirs. But also give meaning and interpretation to the stories through teaching from Scripture, social sciences, and history.

2. Develop a Vibrant Hero System

Second, when seeking to inculcate an adventurous spirituality in your group, find heroes who embody such a spirituality. Any person's or organization's heroes tell us a lot about what they value. Heroes are myth-bearers and therefore transmitters of meaning and belief. Traditionally, prophets, apostles, founders, saints, and martyrs are the church's heroes of the faith. Here are some pointers to developing a vibrant hero system:

Develop a homegrown league of heroes: In creating a culture of adventure, there has to be some collectively agreed-upon "hero system" that defines and symbolizes what is truly valued by the community.

Use many archetypes: Our heroes must include more types than just those who are great at caring for others and/or those who can gather information and communicate well. Certainly these are forms of heroism, but we must broaden out to include the great "doers of the word," spiritual revolutionaries, and other adventurers of the spirit.

Develop a working mythology: Again the stories we tell ourselves embody our mythos. We should learn how to tell the stories of others in ways that develop the hero system of the organization.

Remember, as disciples our archetypal hero is Jesus; and in order to be authentically Christian, our everyday heroes should somehow reflect him.

3. Ritualize Liminality–Communitas

Never underestimate the power of ritual and symbol in the formation of culture. Sociologists are absolutely clear on this—these are not just useful, they are *essential*. Evangelicals need to recover the power of symbol and ritual in general, but in this specific instance we need to learn how to ritualize our experience of liminality and communitas in order to foster a more adventurous spirituality.

Keep continuity with the past: It is vital to see ourselves as part of an ongoing journey started by our heroes in the Scriptures. Discipleship reaches back many thousands of years. We must connect with this through rituals that embody our archetypal imagery of The Great, The Good, and The Holy. For most Westerners, this is going to mean a very clear and comfortable ownership of their Judeo-Christian symbols of transformation.

But make it local: These can and should be complemented by some local, homegrown events and rituals. But remember, great archetypal symbols are not simply created on a weekend outing. Develop a great liminality-communitas tradition over time.

Build it into the ritual life of the church: Develop a regular (yearly?) ritual in the church service where people who have ventured well over that year can be recognized as "heroes" of the community. Liturgy is important if we are to embed liminality-communitas into the life of the faith community. Also, rituals experienced early on often become much more meaningful later in life. So even where much of the more symbolic or theological aspects might go over the heads of some of the younger folk, the hero system that is implied will stick and will hopefully become a functioning part of their mythic universe of meaning.

Formalize the experience for the children: Richard Rohr says that as far as introducing children into the culture, "neither the father and mother, nor any of the leaders of the community, ask the child's permission if he 'wants' to do this. The ideal attitude is that it is expected and to be desired, which must start some years before and eventually exist as a tradition within the family. This lack of 'a tradition of expectation' is much of our problem today, but we have to stick together long enough to create a history for ourselves."[23]

Confer social rewards for local heroes: Certain rights and status should be granted for people who have passed through liturgically recognized liminality-communitas experiences. This might sound elitist, but we know from anthropology that people will not take the proposed idea seriously if rights are conferred cheaply and without accountability.

Create symbols of achievement: Part of the use of symbols can be to indicate that a person has passed the "test." Traditionally, societies have marked the bodies of initiates. Perhaps a tattoo or a necklace or something symbolic can be conferred.

Create a mentor system: It is essential that an intimate mentoring connection be established between the younger and older disciple-adventurers. This allows mutual love and respect to emerge, while transferring status and responsibility within the community. It also creates some sort of formation and preparation in the larger group.

Learn from Hollywood: We can observe from all cultures that initiation rites tend to have a character of mystery and secrecy, both to create necessary anxiety and interest beforehand, and to free from the impossibility of explaining everything afterward. If we take this seriously, then aside from the general terms of time and place, don't tell people a whole lot beforehand, except that they have to experience it to understand it. And afterward, as Heinrich Zimmer says, "the best things cannot be talked about."[24] This creates a sense of expectation, mystery, and intrigue that adds a romantic element to adventure.

We love the way Hope Church in Springfield, Illinois, has developed the following set of criteria for developing communitases in their church.

1. You must care about people who don't know Jesus.
2. Your small group must believe that God can reach the person.
3. Your small group must make a plan.
4. Your small group must overcome difficulties.

5. Your small group needs the courage to do something different.
6. Your small group members must work together to get the job done.
7. Your small group must be willing to pay the cost to bring someone to Jesus.[25]

If we have overstated our case in this chapter, it is because we believe that liminality-communitas is laced throughout our best understandings of life. And we also strongly believe that the church ought to recover this wonderful aspect of what it means to be Jesus's people. If we are able to develop this more vigorous expression of human community, we are sure people in our lost world will be drawn by a desire to be part of a group that is doing something great in the world.

3

A Walk on the Wilder Side

Overcoming Fear in Pursuit of Wild Hope

He who risks and fails can be forgiven. He who never risks and never fails is a failure in his whole being.

—Paul Tillich

The true understanding of the Bible is that it tells us a story of which my life is a part, the story of God's tireless, loving, wrathful, inexhaustible patience with the human family, and of our unbelief, blindness, and disobedience. To accept this story as the truth of the human story (and so my story) commits me personally to a life of discernment and obedience in the new circumstances of each day.

—Lesslie Newbigin

Martin Luther King Jr. once observed that "the only real revolutionary is a person who has nothing to lose."[1] There is a truth to this. Those of us with too much invested in the way things are will never embrace the revolutionary cause required for wholesale change. King's associates were among the most marginalized, disempowered people in America at that time. The same could be said about the associates of the imprisoned Nelson Mandela in South Africa or poverty-stricken Gandhi in India. Free from reliance on the system they sought to overthrow, they were liberated to dedicate themselves to their revolutionary cause. And it is the call to revolution thus defined that is somehow integral to Jesus's various demands regarding discipleship: that his followers submit to the ignominy of a cross (Matt. 10:38; 16:24), to the death of personal agenda (Mark 8:34), and to absolute loyalty to him and his cause (Luke 9:23–26; 14:26, 33).

This submission to the threshold of a cross is at the very root of our following Jesus; it changes the game completely. Now discipleship is not about mere attendance in church meetings; it is about how we develop, mature, learn, adapt, and relate to God. It is about divesting oneself of allegiance to a religious system or institution and embracing the freedom of having nothing to lose. Much of who we are as Jesus's people will depend largely on the quality of our discipleship. A church as Jesus defined it ought to be comprised of disciples and not just admirers, or it hardly is a church.

The Faith of Leap

Philosopher George Santayana wrote, "We don't know who discovered water, but we know it wasn't fish!" Because fish know nothing but water, they would have nothing to compare it to, no other frame of reference, that would help them describe it. Likewise, it seems that defining the nature of faith itself is somewhat difficult for us, because it is just assumed in the God relationship and is therefore largely cognitively invisible to us. What actually *is* faith? And how do we exercise it in ways that change us and the world? Theologians have long pondered this, and many embrace the Reformation theology's definition of a multilayered phenomenon comprising

1. recognition of certain facts about God, the world, self, etc. (*notitia*);
2. the confession of the truth of those facts and that they are somehow authoritative for us (*assensus*); and

3. existentially trusting ourselves to the promises and claims of God that we find in them (*fiducia*).

The first two levels, while necessary, require little from us in terms of personal commitment. Even if facts, theological or otherwise, do imply a certain obligation to live according to them, they don't *in themselves* change us. Any preacher knows this. People live whole lifetimes accumulating facts about God and living lives far from him (Isa. 29:13; Matt. 15:8). Facts in themselves can be acknowledged from "the top of the head" rather than as a response of the whole person to God. Simply reciting a creed before the judgment seat is never going to save anyone. James says, "You believe that there is one God. Good! Even the demons believe that—and shudder" (2:19). Even knowing truths *about* God is not enough to save—the Pharisees had that all pinned down. No, we must actively *risk ourselves* to the truth that we believe is true, and this in turn involves staking our lives on the person and the promises of God.

Seen in this light, faith is the exciting venture in which we bet that God really *is*—that this is his world, and that he is like Jesus Christ, and that he saves those who love him with their lives! It is therefore correct to say, with Elton Trueblood, that "faith is not belief without proof, but is trust without reservation." Therefore faith is more an act of courage than it is an act of knowledge.

We follow Blaise Pascal's dictum that faith is not lazy acceptance of dogma but rather something more akin to a gamble.[2] It is the essence of a gamble that the gambler either wins or loses—he is either right or wrong. We must make our most fundamental decisions in risk, without certain knowledge—we do not see the faces of the cards. This is what it means to "believe." It is the supreme "gamble." C. S. Lewis could say, "If I am sure of anything I am sure that His teaching was never meant to confirm my congenital preference for safe investments and limited liabilities."[3] Or as David Bosch puts it, "Mission is, quite simply, the participation of Christians in the liberating mission of Jesus, wagering on a future that verifiable experience seems to belie."[4] Indeed it is the ultimate wager. Elton Trueblood can therefore rightly say, "Faith, when we think about it, is not merely intellectual assent to a set of propositions, but the supreme gamble in which we stake our lives upon a conviction: It is closer to courage than it is to mere belief."[5]

It is no different when it comes to all our endeavors, including leadership, ministry, and mission, in the world. David Bosch continues, "[Mission] is an altogether ambivalent enterprise executed in the context of tension between divine providence and human confusion. The Church's involvement in mission remains an act of faith without earthly guarantees."[6]

All this to highlight how foundational, indeed how *primal*, risk and courage are to faith itself. And how basic this faith is to salvation, discipleship, spirituality, knowledge of God, and maturity. How is it that we think we can eliminate courage from the Christian life and ever hope to remain faithful? How is it that churches can justify making "safe spaces" by removing faithful risk (*fiducia*) from the equation, substituting it with a whole lot of knowledge (*notitia* and *assensus*), and hope to fulfill the revolutionary commission that we all live under? Martin Luther would be rightfully enraged, because this is what he fought against.

Putting Fear into Perspective

Scott Bader-Saye has written an excellent, timely, and somewhat unique book on the role of fear in culture and in the life of faith.[7] What at first seems like such an odd topic turns out to be a very important one as we tackle the nature of discipleship and witness in our time. The reality is that fear is endemic to the human condition, and while that has always been the case, the culture of fear in which we live actually drives us more than we think. Marketers sell us products that appeal to the economics of fear; and in a post-9/11 world, we are equally driven by the politics of fear. Christians, insofar as we are influenced by the culture in which we live, are certainly not immune. In fact, we seem to exhibit little difference from the non-Christians around about us—and it is not doing our witness much good.

Recently Alan had a startling conversation with two good friends, who, driven by long-term, unnamed, unresolved anxieties, have taken refuge in what can only be called an attitude of fear and loathing.

This manifested in a vitriolic denunciation of illegal immigrants, the refusal to connect with standard wireless internet for fear that someone will maliciously download pornography on their computers, and withdrawal of all their money from the banks. According to these deeply intelligent, sincere, spiritual people, everything has become a conspiracy of socialists, the feds, Obama, European liberals, Muslims, whoever. They believe that America will be forced to split into three separate nations through the activities of the various secessionist movements operating throughout the American Midwest—some of which, according to them, were even considering the possibility of an overthrow, a coup d'état no less, of the American government!

And so the conversation went, most of it deeply irrational and fueled by more homegrown conspiracy theories than you can poke a stick at. Seriously! If the dollar/currency collapses and the banks all close, as they so confidently predict, then cash itself will be worthless because the very concept of money presupposes a functioning economy in the first place! What use will having all your cash stashed under the bed be if it has no value as a means of exchange? Not to mention training one's lovely Christian daughter to use a gun to blow away anyone who gets close to her stash of food and water. Think about that for a while—killing someone because they are thirsty! Bader-Saye is right that suspicion becomes a virtue in the culture of fear. If we assume that we are always "at risk," we will always treat others as potential threats.[8]

Surely this is the kind of "compound mentality" that motivates and energizes cults? Think David Koresh! Ponder the mentality of the Kool-Aid drinkers here. And we have to ask, where exactly is the redeeming power of Jesus in all this? Where is the trust in the gospel's power to overcome sin and despair and the associated call to live confidently in the love of God (Eph. 3:1–21)? What of being willing to give one's life in his name and cause?

This fear-driven paranoia could be dismissed as lunatic fringe except that the two people in view are seriously high-profile, well-regarded Christian leaders! And while they might be on the edge of "normal" in this regard, they do in fact represent something of a mindset evident to greater or lesser degrees throughout American church culture.

While fear is a really dangerous thing, it is not evil *in itself*. It is not wrong to have fears, it is just plain human. But make no mistake: excessive, or what theologians call *disordered*, fear, if not prayerfully brought under Jesus's centering lordship, can lead us directly to vices such as cowardice, apathy, rage, and violence. If left unchecked, untamed fear always draws upon the irrational, evil-tinged sides of human nature. It is not too much to claim that genocides are largely motivated by unresolved fears and anxieties. Theologian Ted Peters, following thinkers like Søren Kierkegaard, Karl Barth, and others, places unresolved fear (of loss, death, possessions, the other, etc.) and unnamed anxieties at the root of all sin and evil—and not without some justification.[9]

Fear causes a kind of contraction of the heart. As such, it inhibits godly actions such as love, hospitality, risky mission, and generosity. For instance, by imagining some future evil, fear draws us in on ourselves so that we refuse to "extend" to people or causes that require sacrifice and risk. This, in turn, becomes a direct barrier to Christian discipleship, which calls us not to contract but to expand, not to limit ourselves to a few things but to open ourselves lovingly and generously to many things, not to attack that which threatens us, but to love even an enemy.[10] Peters writes,

> Fear is a moral issue in so far as it shapes the kind of people we become, and the kind of people we become has a lot to do with how we see the world around us. Our judgments about what is going on in the world and how to interpret events go a long way towards helping us define proper actions. Quite simply, how we view (or interpret) the world shapes how we act in the world.[11]

There is one place in life where fear shows itself in a big way— parents and their kids. The Pixar classic *Finding Nemo* highlights this brilliantly by showing us an example of paranoid parenting, and pointing us to the redemptive aspects of life, adventure, liminality, and communitas. Having lost his wife and a nestful of eggs in a shark attack, the clown fish Marlin makes it his mission in life to preserve his only remaining child, Nemo, from all danger. But Nemo is abducted, and Marlin goes after him. His newfound friend/comrade Dory willingly joins him on his quest to find his son and bring him home. At one point Marlin says to her:

"I promised him I'd never let anything happen to him."
[To which Dory replies,] "Huh. That's a funny thing to promise."
"What?"
"Well, you can't never let anything happen to him. Then nothing would ever happen to him. Not much fun for Little Nemo."

At some point a preoccupation with safety can get in the way of living full lives. Fear can poison a host of good and life-giving activities that we once took for granted, like taking a walk in the woods, playing in the sun, or swimming in the ocean. This is exactly what happens when we parent out of fear. We begin thinking primarily about what we want to prevent and avoid rather than what we want to encourage and develop. But it is not enough to keep our children safe. Parents need to create space for our children to explore and even take risks in the process of growing, learning, and developing. We want our children to grow into adults who are expansive and generous rather than fearful and constricted.[12]

Bader-Saye also notes,

When "good parenting" is replaced by "safe parenting," child rearing is easily captured by consumption—we may not be able to buy goodness, but we can buy safety. And if a given product claims to make your child safer, how do you refrain from buying it without seeming to say, "I'm not interested in my child's safety." Yet where does it end? Being locked in a padded room is very safe, but it's hardly a life.[13]

We need a healthy biblical perspective on fear so we can acknowledge it without being overwhelmed by it, and resist it without assuming we should (or could) live completely fearless lives. At the risk of over-quoting Bader-Saye, he asserts:

This is especially important among Christians who seek to follow Jesus, for Jesus's words, and more so his life, do not promise safety. Following the teachings of Jesus will involve us in risky practices like clothing the naked, visiting the prisoner, caring for the sick, welcoming the stranger, and feeding the hungry (see Matt. 25:31–46). Following the life of Jesus will mean walking in the way of the cross, the way of "self-giving love." The apostle Paul describes this vocation in his second letter to the Corinthians, "For while we live, we are always being given up to death for Jesus' sake, so that the life of Jesus may be made visible in our mortal flesh" (2 Cor. 4:11). Such risky discipleship can hardly be described as "safe." . . . Faith must be daring, because following Jesus is risky. . . . Fear makes it difficult to embrace the vulnerability involved in discipleship.[14]

The Bible claims that the "fear of the Lord is the beginning of wisdom" (Ps. 111:10; Prov. 1:7; 2:5; Acts 9:31) and for good reason. It is probably the only fear that will not cripple us. Because "wisdom" is the ordering of life in accord with God's will, appropriate fear of God is the only thing that gives us the right perspective of, and puts us into right relationship with, the objects of our perception. Holy reverence is therefore the right basis for coping with life's meaning and problems. *Here* lies our much-needed perspective. From a biblical point of view, there is nothing neurotic about fearing God. The neurotic thing is *not* to fear God, or to be afraid of the many other wrong things we tend to fear. "That is why God chooses to be known to us, so that we may stop being afraid of the wrong things. When God is fully revealed to us and we 'get it,' then we experience the conversion of our fear."[15] "For God has not given us a spirit of fear, but of power and of love and of a sound mind" (2 Tim. 1:7 NKJV). And so we discover that the fear of God, rather than being a repressive cringing from the intrusion of the Divine in our lives, turns out to be an unexpected gateway to the true love of God. This is the beginning of wisdom. And here is our much-needed perspective.

The Church's Role

One of the roles of the church in all this must be to keep encouraging us all to live courageous lives in the gospel, to remain open-ended, and to call us to ongoing comradeship in God's adventure. But the church doesn't always accomplish this. Unless we are very careful to maintain authentic gospel perspectives in these matters, church can easily become the locus of our collective insecurities and its function downgraded to being the last line of moral defense in an immoral world.

Church plays a critical role in the liminal process of cultivating an adventurous faith to replace our fears. But, so often it is otherwise; Robert Capon wittily observes that the church, by and large, has had a poor record of encouraging freedom. She has spent so much time inculcating in us the fear of making mistakes that she has made us like ill-taught piano students: we play our songs, but we never hear them because our main concern is not to make music but to avoid some mistake that will get us into trouble.[16]

This is what we mean by "compound mentality," where the church becomes the last refuge of fearful people who believe that the whole world is plotting our demise. But this is an abdication of what it really means to be the church that Jesus built! If the brave, loving life and sacrificial death of Jesus (and the apostolic church, and other great movements, for that matter) teach us anything, it is that his cause cannot be defeated by sin and evil—heck, he is the one who defeated sin in the first place! And his church ought to be the one place where this triumph is clearly on display for all to see (Eph. 2:14–22; Col. 2:13–15). "You, dear children, are from God and have overcome them, because the one who is in you is greater than the one who is in the world" (1 John 4:4). And lest you think that the church is a defensive unit, just remember that it's the gates of hell that don't hold up against our advances . . . not the other way around (Matt. 16:18)!

By taking our eyes off the ball, or anxiously focusing on technique, orderly worship, political correctness, or whatever, we not only lose focus, we also miss the point of what it is all about. Only Christians who refuse to be infected by the neurotic anxieties so prevalent in our age will have any hope of exercising missional impact on the surrounding culture. Such disciples will not scorn the anxieties of other people but will show them how to extricate themselves from fears and will point out the paths by which they can step out into the open—"into faith's daring."[17]

A Vision Bigger Than Our Fears

But we all know that we can't simply command ourselves to feel less fear, can we? What we can do is allow the fears themselves to be overwhelmed by bigger and better things—by a sense of adventure and the fullness of life that comes from relocating our fears and vulnerabilities within the larger story that is ultimately hopeful and not tragic.[18] And we can thereby learn what it means to live, learn, and love in Jesus's name.

There is no doubt that to walk with Jesus means to walk on the wilder side of life. Spirituality and discipleship in the Way of Jesus *is* demanding, but it is also God's blueprint for an authentic life of wholesome (holy) humanity. But let's face it, not many of us take this journey, or at least we do it only halfheartedly. Wherever we are required to reach down into our innermost recesses, into the heart of personality, we think it too risky, and so most of us are overcome by fear, and many run away. The life well lived, the adventure of discipleship, therefore remains a half-experience, relegated largely to the youthful years. English novelist Mary Cholmondeley says that "every day I live I am more convinced that the waste of life lies in the love we have not given, the powers we have not used, the selfish prudence that will risk nothing and which, shirking pain, misses happiness as well."[19]

So how do we recapture in a deeply personal way that primal love that makes us whole, that passion that drives us onto the streets and into the neighborhoods, that life we sense is being lived to the full? Part of the answer lies in overcoming our fears as described above. It also means learning to love, breaking the cloying cultural constraints that have hemmed us in, and overcoming our aversion to risk.

Of all these, love is the greatest (1 Cor. 13:13).

Loving Love

Starting from the biblical revelation, saints as well as psychologists of all persuasions affirm that people need to love and learn how to love if they are to grow into mature human beings. In *ReJesus* and again in *Untamed*,[20] we asserted that all Christian spirituality can be traced back to Jesus's complete (re)affirmation of the *shema*—the unavoidable call to live a life of wholeness under the One True God, loving him with heart, soul, mind, strength, and loving one's neighbors as oneself. According to our Lord, there are no higher obligations to God, no greater spirituality, than this duty to live a life of multidimensional love (Mark 12:29–31).

Learning to love, and therefore becoming mature, is no mean feat. It requires putting oneself on the line and embracing the risk, even likelihood, of pain and suffering. There is no way around this; St. Augustine is right when he notes in his confessions that every new love contains "the seeds of fresh sorrows."[21] Our most perceptive thinkers have known this all along, and actually, except for the more sociopathic personality, we ourselves know this only too well. We feel it every time we put our hearts on the line. C. S. Lewis perhaps best captures this tragic element in love with these unforgettable words of insight and warning:

> Love anything, and your heart will certainly be wrung and possibly be broken. If you want to make sure of keeping it intact, you must give your heart to no one, not even to an animal. Wrap it carefully round with hobbies and little luxuries; avoid all entanglements; lock it up safe in the casket or coffin of your selfishness. But in that casket—safe, dark, motionless, airless—it will change. It will not be broken; instead it will become unbreakable, impenetrable, irredeemable. The alternative to tragedy, or at least to the risk of tragedy, is damnation. The only place outside Heaven where you can be perfectly safe from all the dangers and perturbations [disturbances] of love is Hell.[22]

To love is to suffer . . . and that's probably why we generally don't do it well. Unwillingness to venture, plus a desire to be safe, holds us back from love. To be sure, most of us do have a vision of what makes for a good life, and as believers we know that it involves growing in the love of God. What we seem to lack, however, is the will to attain this good life of love. Most of us prefer to skip over the pain and the discipline, to find some easy, off-the-shelf ways to sainthood. Christian self-help spiritualities are a classic dodge of the real issues and manifestly do not produce maturity. We do well to be reminded of the cost of shortcuts in Carl Jung's penetrating statement, "Neurosis is always a substitute for legitimate suffering."[23]

In his classic novel *The Shoes of the Fisherman*, Australian author Morris West writes:

> It costs so much to be a full human being that there are very few who have the enlightenment or the courage to pay the price. One has to abandon altogether the search for security and reach out to the risk of living with both arms outstretched. One has to embrace the world like a lover. One has to accept pain as a condition of existence. One

has to court doubt at the cost of knowing. One needs a will stubborn in conflict but apt always to total acceptance of every consequence of living and dying.[24]

As extreme and destabilizing as Morris West's statement appears at first, we all sense the truth in it. Love is risky stuff to be sure; it requires moral courage and willful commitment, and will take us on an adventure deep into God's world far away from our narrow self-concerns. As C. S. Lewis notes, even the most lawless and inordinate loves are less contrary to God's will than a self-invited and self-protective lovelessness.[25] In the end it *is* better, and much more human, to have loved and lost than not to have loved at all. Why? Because "God is love. Whoever lives in love lives in God, and God in him" (1 John 4:16).

Wild at Heart

This phrase, made famous by John Eldredge in his book by the name,[26] became a catchcry for the journey that men must make in order to recover a full masculinity. Mark Twain wryly commented that "most men die at 27; we just bury them at 72." Whatever the reasons, this idea does have amazing resonance. When Alan tweeted this quote recently, there were over 300 retweets in one day, and it started a massive discussion on Facebook. People today do feel a death of something essential, an experience of being domesticated.

Whatever the cause, this cultural suppression of the spirit of adventure creates the conditions for either the repressed masculine anger that so readily erupts in male violence or the inverted feminine rage that can appear as self-hatred. While speaking of maleness, writers like Robert Bly, John Eldredge, and Richard Rohr affirm the need to recover the wildly holy, passionate, warrior-like aspect in order to grow into the image that God made them to be.[27] But this is not only an issue of masculinity. All Christians, male and female, must recover what it means to be wild at heart—holy warriors.

We would commend such similar wild energy for women. And so, we believe, do many women. How else do we account for the immensely popular feminist book *Women Who Run with the Wolves*, written long before Eldredge's *Wild at Heart*?[28] Author Clarissa Estes maintains,

Healthy wolves and healthy women share certain psychic characteristics: keen sensing, playful spirit, and a heightened capacity for
devotion. [They] are relational by nature, inquiring, possessed of
great endurance and strength . . . they are fiercely stalwart and very
brave. Yet both have been hounded and harassed. . . . They have been
the targets of those who would clean up the wilds.[29]

Part of this "cleaning up the wilds" comes from a culture designed
to make us all passive units of consumption. "The Matrix" of middle-
class suburbia, with its shopping malls, schools, and single-family
houses complete with massive entertainment systems, is designed
to keep us subservient and unquestioning. But it's a largely invisible
enemy, and it's written through our internal cultural coding—our
"software," so to speak. In this cultural script, the vision of the
good life is reduced to being a highly brand-aware, conspicuous
consumer, rather than being someone whose life should count for
something, who makes a difference in the world. Maybe we all need
to learn to run with the wolves again. Douglas Coupland spoke for
a generation when he said,

> You see, when you're middle class, you have to live with the fact that
> history will ignore you. You have to live with the fact history can
> never champion your causes and that history will never feel sorry for
> you. It is the price that is paid for day-to-day comfort and silence.
> And because of this price, all happinesses are sterile; all sadnesses
> go unpitied.[30]

Agreeing with this, Stephen Lyng, in his book *Edgework*, suggests
that despite the propensity to anesthetize ourselves against danger
with middle-class consumption, we can rarely remain satisfied in that
place. Referring to risk-taking and adventurous behavior as "edgework," he reminds us that all the attractions of modern middle-class
suburban living don't compare to true adventure (or edgework). He
says, "New means of consumption create spectacular environments
and experiences for people looking to escape the stultifying environments of daily work life. But few of these settings and consumption
activities can match the transcendent experience of edgework."[31]

If only the church could believe this and recognize that rather than
sacralizing materialism and baptizing consumption, they should

provide that "transcendent experience" of liminality and adventure, calling their members out of middle-class safety and into mission. But the standard churchy spirituality does not require any real action, courage, or sacrifice from its attendees. Church attendance, tithing, Bible study, and worship are all genuinely good things but, separated as they are from the more active, liminal forms of spirituality, tend to add to the already stultifying passivity we already feel. True biblical spirituality must always strain against any drift to mere social conformity as if it were (God forbid) some form of inevitable fact we all eventually have to come to grips with. If that were the case, then Coupland's tragic description applies equally to the average "church attendee." The very phrase *church attendee*, while a fitting description of how so many understand the demands of Christianity, is an insult to the kind of lifestyle that Jesus wants from us.

The church of Jesus needs to wake up from the exile of passivity and embrace liminality and adventure or continue to remain a religious ghetto for culturally co-opted, fearful, middle-class folk. Our very souls are at stake.

The Educational Aspects of Adventure

Peter Drucker said that people who *don't* take risks generally make about two big mistakes a year, and that people who *do* take risks generally make about two big mistakes a year. If he is right in this, then why would we not be people who take the risks? At least we will learn from failure in the process. If we never risk failure, we will never succeed—even in the smallest things. We do well to remember the parable of the talents in this regard; it ends with this warning: "For everyone who has will be given more, and he will have an abundance. Whoever does not have, even what he has will be taken from him" (Matt. 25:14–29). Surely it's better to spend whatever gifts we have been given by God in faithful risk-taking than fearfully hide them away. If we fail, at least we will fail faithfully and not fearfully.

All this raises the role of liminality in learning and education. To return to Lyng's seminal book on the sociology of risk, *Edgework*,[32] the authors describe a certain kind of knowledge available only at the edge, or in our language, in the liminal space. It's the kind of learning that can occur only in more extreme contexts and is pretty much captured in this quote from American novelist Louisa May Alcott: "I'm not afraid of storms, for I'm learning how to sail my ship."[33] The storm is an essential element in learning how to sail a ship. It is also perhaps the reason why, for instance, the Grand Prix competition is the primary seedbed for innovation in auto-engineering. The liminal contexts of learning provoke new insights on old themes. This "edge" intelligence is sometimes difficult for edgeworkers to describe, largely because it is so experiential, but it yields conceptual insights that cannot be gained otherwise.

Kurt Hahn, the great educator, understood the importance of liminality for edgework when he pioneered what is called "expeditionary learning," a form of education that has been used to develop people of all ages and in every continent. Expeditionary learning uses adventurous (liminal) experiences to create situations of learning, and so the principles are useful for us here.

1. *The primacy of self-discovery*: Learning happens best with emotion, challenge, and the requisite support. People discover their abilities, values, passions, and responsibilities in situations that offer adventure and the unexpected. In the situations created by expeditionary learning, learners undertake tasks that require perseverance, fitness, craftsmanship, imagination, self-discipline, and significant achievement. A teacher's primary task in such situations is to help students overcome their fears and discover they can do more than they think they can.

2. *Generating and testing viable ideas*: In situations of liminality and risk, innovation inevitably occurs. Here the role of teaching is to foster curiosity about the world by creating learning situations that provide something important to think about, time to experiment, and time to make sense of what is observed.

3. *The personal and social responsibility for learning*: In liminal situations we discover that learning is both a personal process of discovery and a social activity. Everyone learns both individually and as part of a group. Every aspect of the learning process encourages both participants to become increasingly responsible for directing their own personal and collective learning.

4. *Empathy and caring*: Liminality creates the conditions where people learn to have each other's backs. Learning is fostered best in communities where learners' as well as teachers' ideas are respected and where there is mutual trust. Expeditionary learning promotes the extensive use of small groups and personal mentors while in the situation of adventure.

5. *Learning from success and failure*: Because the situation places the learners at risk, they learn vital lessons from failure as well as success. All students need to be successful if they are to build the confidence and capacity to take risks and meet increasingly difficult challenges. But it is also important for students to learn from their failures, to persevere when things are hard, and to learn to turn disabilities into opportunities.

6. *Collaboration and competition*: In expeditionary learning, individual and group development are integrated so that the value of friendship, trust, and group action is clear. Learners are encouraged to compete not against each other but with their own personal best and with rigorous standards of excellence.

7. *Diversity and inclusion*: Both diversity and inclusion increase the richness of ideas, creative power, problem-solving ability, and respect for others. In expeditionary learning, learners investigate and value their different histories and talents as well as those of other communities and cultures. Learning groups are therefore heterogeneous.

8. *Learning from creation*: A direct and respectful relationship with the natural world refreshes the human spirit and teaches the important ideas of recurring cycles and organic rhythms. Because they are in touch with real conditions of life and nature, learners become stewards of the earth and of future generations.

9. *Solitude and reflection*: Students and teachers need time alone to explore their own thoughts, make their own connections, and create their own ideas. They also need time to compare notes and share their reflections with others. The relative lulls in the adventure experience create perfect conditions for such reflective learning.

10. *Service and compassion*: All, teachers and students alike, are crew and no one is allowed to be a passenger—all are participants. Everyone is strengthened by acts of significant service to

others, and one of expeditionary learning's primary functions is to instill in learners the attitudes and skills to learn from and be of service to others.[34]

We can all learn and develop in such situations, and the church can be more effective in developing disciples that can make an impact in their world. To these we add some further principles to engender learning and innovation.

1. Foster Pioneering and Protest

Genuine learning and advancement in the church, as in all aspects of life, will generally be led by a few people who are willing to break from the herd instincts of the crowd. If we are going to be innovative in mission, we will need to foster a pioneering spirit because, as we have seen, more of the same is not going to get the job done.

Pioneers have to be a particularly hardy bunch. New social and religious movements inevitably arise as a protest against the status quo, which in turn arouses sometimes stern opposition from the system from which they emerge (e.g., the Celts and the Roman Catholics, Francis and the popes, Wesley and Booth and the Anglicans, Martin Luther King and the civil rights movement, etc.). Machiavelli was not far wrong when he said, "Nothing is more difficult to carry out, nor more doubtful of success, nor more dangerous to handle, than achieving a new order of things."[35] Would-be innovator-reformers will have adversaries who directly benefit from the old order and halfhearted defenders (lukewarm largely because of fear of the adversaries) who would benefit from the new. It's the reason why prophets and apostles are almost always persecuted and tend to stand alone.

At all turning points in history, when the older forms are dying, new possibilities are created by a few people who are not afraid to stand out and risk security. Susan B. Anthony, the remarkable civil rights activist and pioneer of the women's suffrage movement in the United States, knew this all too well. Speaking from experience, she said,

> Cautious, careful people always casting about to preserve their reputation and social standing, never can bring about a reform. Those who are really in earnest must be willing to be anything or nothing in the world's estimation, and publicly and privately, in season and

95

out, avow their sympathy with despised and persecuted ideas and their advocates, and bear the consequences.[36]

She could have been talking here about St. Patrick, Martin Luther, Nelson Mandela, or Gandhi—or Jesus, for that matter. All genuine reformers tend to suffer for their cause. In order to develop a pioneering missional spirit, a capacity for genuine ecclesial innovation, let alone engender daring discipleship, we are going to need the capacity to take a courageous stand when and where necessary.

2. Stir Up Holy Discontent

Karl Marx said that, in order to foster revolution, activists will need to "rub raw the sores of discontent." He understood that people would not pay the price for change unless they felt a profound sense of disgruntlement with the prevailing conditions. Now we think this is a highly manipulative thing to do in the context of a political revolution, but this should not obscure the redeemable truth that lies behind this approach—discontent results in movement and movement in change. Or, in the interests of a holy revolution, we have got to cultivate a *holy* discontent in our own hearts and in our systems if we are going to move toward a better future. Speaking of our spiritual yearnings, Jewish theologian/philosopher Abraham Heschel says, "All that is creative stems from the seed of endless discontent. . . . He who is satisfied has never truly craved."[37] In order to engender change in our lives, especially in organizations, we have to *sell the problem before we sell the solution*.

But holy discontent need not always be the result of a prophetic critique of things; it could come about from a holy sense of curiosity and being attentive to the provocatively fertile nature of good, probing questions. As discussed in the introduction, we ought never to take ourselves out of the questing aspect of Christianity and discipleship. Spiritual quests in particular are driven by the need for a deeper, more satisfying experience of life and faith. Questing is the result of holy discontent, and more often than not, as in all genuine renewal movements, it is the result of the Holy Spirit working directly in our lives. And behind every good quest lies at least one really good question—we do well to heed Einstein's advice to a young admirer when he said, "The important thing is to not stop questioning. Curiosity has its own reason for existence."[38]

3. Trade Your Traditionalism for Tradition

While it is true to say what got you *here* won't get you *there*, genuine learning is not done in a historical vacuum, and innovation is not simply novelty. Some of our best expressions of adventurous church have been movements that exist in our past and form part of our historical tradition. In *The Forgotten Ways* Alan suggested that every church already has all it needs to get the job done—in other words, we have latent potentials, and through disuse or misuse, we have simply forgotten how to activate them. Part of our learning then is not simply coming up with faddish ideas, but recovering the deepest identity and potentials that *we already have* as God's people. Becoming the church that Jesus built will require courage, because it means letting go of what we have become . . . of abandoning the security of institutional church to become a movement.

At the conclusion of the musical *Fiddler on the Roof*, the question is asked, "What holds him [the Fiddler] up?" The answer the audience hears is "Tradition." But being guided by tradition and being traditionalist are two entirely different things. The tradition*ist* is the institutional persecutor of change and will subvert the missional cause. Intransigent and closed to the spirit, they lazily rely on the past successes of those who have paved the way before them. Tradition, on the other hand, involves being sensitive to the fact that we have a long history and we don't operate in a vacuum. *Paradosis*, the Greek word for tradition, means "to hand down." The creativity of "fiddling around" is possible when it is done within the ongoing self-consciousness of being part of the ancient people of God. What we do now has a past as much as it has a future. It is this sense of identity handed down through time that gives us the imagery and the security to think the new. Undoubtedly the best way to preserve tradition is to have children, not wear your father's old hat (attributed to Picasso).

4. Be Willing to Fail Forward

Trial and error is one of the most basic ways of learning. So much so that Albert Einstein, arguably the greatest scientist ever, once said,

> Anyone who has never made a mistake has never tried anything new. Besides the practical knowledge that defeat offers, there are important personality benefits gained in the process. Defeat strips away false values and makes you realize what you really want.[39]

It means that when something fails, we have to let go of ideas we have become attached to or that have somehow attached themselves to us.

One of the greatest qualities in adventurous learners is that they have learned to *fail forward*. In his book *Failing Forward*, John Maxwell writes that there are seven key abilities that allow successful people to fail forward instead of taking each setback personally.[40] According to him, "successful" people:

Reject rejection: Successful people don't blame themselves when they fail. They take responsibility for each setback, but they don't take the failure personally.

View failure as temporary: "People who personalize failure see a problem as a hole they're permanently stuck in," writes Maxwell. "But achievers see any predicament as temporary."

View each failure as an isolated incident: Successful people don't define themselves by individual failures. They recognize that each setback is a small part of the whole.

Have realistic expectations: Too many people start big projects with the unrealistic expectation that they'll see immediate results. Success takes time. When you pursue anything worthwhile, there are going to be bumps along the way. And remember: the perfect is the enemy of the good.

Focus on strengths: If you operate from your weaknesses you are going to fail time and again. To be sure, you must not allow weaknesses to undermine you, but work from the basis of your strengths.

Vary approaches: Adventurers are willing to vary their approaches to problems. If one approach doesn't work for you, if it brings repeated failure, then try something else. To fail forward, you must do what works for you, not necessarily what works for other people.

Bounce back: Finally, successful people are resilient. They don't let one error keep them down. They learn from their mistakes and move on. To paraphrase Edward de Bono, it is better to have enough ideas for some of them to be wrong, than to be always right by having no ideas at all.[41]

Stakeholding

One other principle of liminality should be factored into our equation. We call it the stakeholder principle. It is the idea that all the players in a project ought to have a direct stake in the outcomes, because if strategic choices don't fundamentally impact us *personally*, it is unlikely we will make decisions with the kind of seriousness they deserve. We need to act as if our lives depended on it.

When all our church ever expects from us is attendance and tithing, we hardly feel as though our lives are at stake. Indeed, in medium- to large-sized churches, many people suspect their attendance and tithing wouldn't really be missed. In those churches where the Sunday meeting is the primary project, most members know the show will go on with or without them. This can hardly be called stakeholding, and once members work that out, they find all sorts of excuses for attending only every other week, or every three weeks, or less. In this respect, as we identified in our first book together, *The Shaping of Things to Come*, most churches are mainly audiences, and any member of an audience is dispensable. As soon as you know you're dispensable, the impetus for attendance is lost. After all, the play will still be performed even if half the theatre seats are unoccupied. However, the play cannot be performed if any of the cast is absent—or if performed, it is diminished in some way by the absence of that cast member. Actors in a repertory company are stakeholders in that company.

Liminal churches are more like repertory theatre companies than their audiences, and as a result they know the powerful sense of connection with each other—that camaraderie—that won't allow any member to let the others down. For the rep company, the common ordeal they face is opening night. For a liminal church, there needs to be a similarly common ordeal, and everyone needs to be committed to owning that challenge collectively. Without significant levels of buy-in or stakeholding by the team, the possibility of significant levels of innovation and energy are reduced. This is only exacerbated when considering the role of the leaders.

Alan learned this very painfully in one of his missional adventures when he opened Elevation, a café and nightclub in Melbourne, as a missional proximity space in 2001.[42] A risky venture (it was an innovative start-up in a highly competitive field), it eventually failed, costing a lot of money and having a damaging impact on the church that was involved. On reflection, one of the biggest mistakes made was in hiring a manager rather than engaging a stakeholding partner in that role. The manager, a hireling, was empowered to make serious decisions on a daily basis, but had no real stake in the business—or as Americans say, he had "no skin in the game." He was basically in a "job." If it failed, then no worries, he could easily seek another one. And that's exactly what happened. It got tough and he left at a critical time, leaving the partners in one big mess. Alan swore never to make the same mistake again. The learning: in all major projects people who make decisions about the future of the venture should somehow hold stakes in the outcomes. If all goes well, they win; if it does not go well, they lose some skin along with the other stakeholders.

Burn the Boats!

In 1519, with some 600 men, 16 or so horses, and 11 boats, Hernán Cortés landed on a vast inland plateau now called Mexico. They had come from Spain to the New World in search of some of the world's greatest treasure. But, with only 600 men with no protective armor, conquering an empire so extensive was a highly unlikely affair.

Instead of charging through cities and forcing his men into immediate battle, Cortés stayed on the beach and awoke the souls of his men with emblazoned speeches ingeniously designed to urge on the spirit of adventure and invoke a thirst for lifetimes of fortune amongst his troops. His orations bore fruit, for what was supposedly a military exploit now took on an extravagant romance in the imaginations of the troops. Ironically, it was not the eloquent "preaching" that led to the ultimate victory of those adventurers; it was just three words that would change the history of the New World. As they marched inland to face their enemies, Cortés ordered, "Burn the boats!" They did, and thereby eradicated any possibility of retreat from the minds of the troops. They had to commit themselves unwaveringly to the cause—win or die. Retreat was no longer an option.

Putting aside the violent nature of the example above (the conquistadors were cruel and rapacious colonizers), we can observe the power of the *no turning back* approach to innovation in the story of Cortés and his conquistadors. Troy Tyler, a very successful entrepreneur, says it this way: "Strategy is all about commitment. If what you're doing isn't irrevocable, then you don't have a strategy—because anyone can do it. . . . I've always wanted to treat life like I was an invading army and there was no turning back."[43] When there is no possibility of retreat, we will find the innovation that only the liminal situation can bring. In short, we find the faith of leap. Or, as the novelist Katherine Mansfield put it, "Whenever I prepare for a journey I prepare as though for death. Should I never return, all is in order."[44]

4

The Hero's Journey

Becoming Who We Were Made to Be

It is only in adventure that some people succeed in knowing themselves.

—André Gide

It is my desire, in the office of a Christian minister, to do nothing which I cannot do with my whole heart. Having said this, I have said all.

—Ralph Waldo Emerson

The conversion and subsequent mission of Patrick to the Irish peoples started one of the most remarkable movements in the history of the church, a movement destined to "save civilization" and embed the gospel in the West. One of the slogans of this remarkable movement was "the cell and the coracle." This strange phrase actually refers to the two central aspects/rhythms of the Celtic movement. The "cell" refers to the place of contemplative prayer—where the monks and nuns spent time alone before God as well as in community worship. The notion of the cell as central to the life of the Irish monastics captures well the profound commitment to intimacy with God that was reflected in their leaders of the movement (Patrick, Aidan, Brendan, etc.).

The "coracle," on the other hand, describes a round, keelless, flat-bottomed boat made from woven wood covered in skins or canvas and waterproofed with tar. While it was expected that all members of the movement have a rich life of worship and prayer—as would be presumed with monastics—it was also expected that all would be involved in the mission to evangelize Ireland, Britain, and Europe. One of the bravest things the Celts did was something we, in our culture of fear, would probably call plain *foolhardy*. About four of them would get into these little boats where they would pray something like this: "Lord of the wind and the waves, take us your servants to where you will." Then, trusting themselves to the sovereign God and his desire to redeem all peoples, they would push out into the ocean, allowing the tides to sweep them up and, hopefully, to land them on some shore where they would then proceed to preach the gospel to the people there! Talk about the faith of leap! With such zealous devotion and commitment to God and his mission, no wonder the Celtic Movement is credited with evangelizing Western Europe during the Dark Ages.

This kind of commitment to God and gospel harks back to Jesus (and the other biblical heroes) of course, but it has particular roots in the life and ministry of St. Paul. Undoubtedly, Paul is one of the most remarkable spiritual heroes of all time. The sheer quality of his character, the focus of his life, the passion of his spirituality, and the creative brilliance of his theology have changed the world forever. Other than Jesus, who has a unique and founding role, Paul is *the* apostle of the church. We must remember that apostles are primarily pioneering idea-missionaries who advance the gospel onto new ground and at the same time provide meaningful leadership for movements. But at the core, the nonnegotiable task of the biblical apostles was to guard and maintain the missionary impulses of the church.[1]

In pursuit of this task then, one of the most powerful metaphors of Paul's missionary journeys is that of the scarlet track of a bleeding hare across the snow. The image, first employed in a sermon by John Henry Jowett, of a startling red slash across the whitened landscape reminds us that Paul's ministry was one of constant self-emptying. This brave, rather unlikely hero led his band of spiritual warriors to and fro across the Roman Empire, all the while bleeding for their cause, the redemption of that very empire. What he experiences along the way is extreme and relentless liminality. But in the same process he also gets as close to God as a man can get (2 Cor. 12:1–5; Phil. 3:7–11), he reframes theological thinking for all time, and he starts a transformative movement of the gospel of Jesus into the Greco-Roman world that extends down through the corridors of time to this very time and place in which we stand.

Even before he began any of his missionary campaigns, Paul was no stranger to high adventure. Soon after his conversion, he had been forced to escape quite dramatically from Damascus after hearing of a conspiracy to kill him. By the time he embarked on what is now known as the first missionary journey, he had spent time in retreat in Arabia, led the church in Antioch, and debated the apostle Peter in Jerusalem. But when we read about his three missionary journeys (Acts 13–14; 15b–18a; 18b–21 respectively), we are introduced to a man who (with various companions) provides a pretty unique insight into the anatomy of spiritual heroism.

The early church was founded upon the images of Paul and his compatriots trekking mountain paths, taking beatings, enduring imprisonment and trials, contending with riots, surviving earthquakes, debating scholars and wizards, upsetting businessmen and religious leaders, as well as planting churches, preaching the gospel, and healing the sick. They formed the blueprint for the earliest models of Christian mission, models that presupposed risk, movement, energy, opposition, and triumph. Paul summarizes his experience for the Corinthians when again he feels compelled to defend his position as an apostle:

> I have worked much harder, been in prison more frequently, been flogged more severely, and been exposed to death again and again. Five times I received from the Jews the forty lashes minus one. Three times I was beaten with rods, once I was stoned, three times I was shipwrecked, I spent a night and a day in the open sea, I have been constantly on the move. I have been in danger from rivers, in danger

from bandits, in danger from my own countrymen, in danger from Gentiles; in danger in the city, in danger in the country, in danger at sea; and in danger from false brothers. I have labored and toiled and have often gone without sleep; I have known hunger and thirst and have often gone without food; I have been cold and naked. (2 Cor. 11:23–27)

And while reading this passage is as uncomfortable as it is exhausting, we should remember that Paul, who had his faults, also maintained a ministry that spanned thirty years and was not all blood, sweat, and tears. There were times of relative stability, real joy in the gospel, deep comradeship in ministry, churches planted and disciples developed, and long periods in prison, which for him, at least, meant productive writing time.

It's fair to say that Paul led an unusually full and adventurous life! His missionary journeys, his time in the coracle so to speak, were times of death-defying adventure. The details of these journeys are well known to many readers, but they bear repeating to remind us that from the outset of the Christian movement, risk and adventure were central to the church's understanding of mission. Taken as a whole, here is a life well lived . . . one worthy of study and emulation. He tells us to imitate him as he follows Christ (1 Cor. 4:16; 11:1). Paul is and remains a lasting symbol of spiritual heroism and model of Christlike discipleship.

Heroes are important not only because they symbolize what we believe to be important, but because they also convey universal truths about personal self-discovery and self-transcendence, one's role in society, and the relation between the two. We can do with more heroes like Paul and the Celtic missionaries around in our day.

The Hero with a Thousand Faces

Paul's letters are like dispatches from the Front, and it is impossible to fully appreciate his ecclesiology without noting the soil from which it grew—adventure and risk under the guiding hand of God. Unfortunately, as we've noted, so much of that sense of adventure is gone from the experience of local churches.

When trying to understand the nature of adventure, we can't help but turn to the acknowledged expert in the field of myth and myth-making, Joseph Campbell. In 1949, Campbell published *The Hero with a Thousand Faces*. For what was essentially a piece of esoteric comparative mythology, it struck a surprisingly deep chord with readers. It has become a twentieth-century nonfiction classic, coming to prominence in popular culture with the release of George Lucas's Star Wars films, which Lucas claimed were inspired by Campbell. Campbell proposed the theory that important myths from around the world and throughout the ages all share a fundamental structure, which he termed the *mono-myth*. Whether they be ancient stories like those of the samurai from Japan, or the Maori warrior stories from New Zealand, or more contemporary stories like the heroic cowboy myth from the American West, Campbell contended that they are all essentially telling the same storyline: that of the hero's journey.

Campbell summarized the mono-myth as follows:

> A hero ventures forth from the world of common day into a region of supernatural wonder: fabulous forces are there encountered and a decisive victory is won: the hero comes back from this mysterious adventure with the power to bestow boons on his fellow man.[2]

But there's much more to it than that. Campbell had exegeted hundreds of myths from around the world and from every epoch of human history, and he kept finding the same structure. The take-home message? Everyone loves to hear this story. Always. And what interests us is the fact that at its core, this mono-myth is a story of heroism and adventure.

It should be no surprise that the world's great myth-makers and storytellers—Hollywood—eventually got interested in Campbell's writings. In the late 1980s, Disney screenwriter Christopher Vogler read Campbell and was so taken by the simplicity of his ideas that he sent out a now legendary seven-page company memo for all Disney screenwriters, entitled "A Practical Guide to *The Hero with a Thousand Faces*." The logic was simple. If people resonate with this story, and can't seem to get enough of it, let's give it to them as often as we can. In the memo, and the subsequent book, *The Writer's Journey*, Vogler simplified Campbell's hero myth into the following twelve stages:

1. Ordinary World—the hero's normal world before the story begins;
2. Call to Adventure—the hero is presented with a problem, challenge, or adventure;
3. Refusal of the Call—the hero refuses the challenge or journey, usually because he's scared or wounded by previous experiences in some way;
4. Meeting with the Mentor—the hero meets a mentor to gain advice or training for the adventure;
5. Crossing the First Threshold—the hero leaves the Ordinary World and goes into the Special World;
6. Tests, Allies, Enemies—the hero faces tests, meets allies, confronts enemies, and learns the rules of the Special World;
7. Approach—the hero has hit setbacks during tests and may need to try a new idea;
8. Ordeal—the biggest life-or-death crisis;
9. Reward—the hero has survived death, overcomes his fear, and now earns the reward;
10. The Road Back—the hero must return to the Ordinary World;
11. Resurrection Hero—another test where the hero faces death—he has to use everything he's learned;
12. Return with Elixir—the hero returns from the journey with the "elixir," and uses it to help everyone in the Ordinary World.[3]

With this list, you can describe just about every Hollywood movie that attains blockbuster status.

If this looks a tad complex, it is worth noting that Campbell himself believed few myths contain all of these stages—some contain most of the stages, while others contain only some of them. Whatever the details, the stages may be organized into three main sections: *Departure* (sometimes called *Separation*), *Initiation*, and *Return*. Departure deals with the hero venturing forth on the quest, Initiation deals with the hero's various adventures along the way, and Return deals with the hero's return home with knowledge and powers acquired on the journey.

At the point of rediscovering the power of their own myth-making through reading Campbell, the Disney studio was on the ropes. It hadn't produced a hit since the Herbie the Volkswagon films of the late '70s. Once the Vogler memo went out and writers deliberately started using the structure of Campbell's mono-myth, Disney released *Honey, I Shrunk the Kids* and *The Little Mermaid* in 1989 and followed that with *Beauty and the Beast* (1991), *Aladdin* (1992), *The Lion King* (1994), and *Toy Story* (1995). They were back in the game.

Each of those films sticks very closely to Vogler's distillation of Campbell's hero myth. For example, in *The Lion King*, young Simba finds himself in the idyllic world of the Pride Lands of the Serengeti, oblivious to the challenges that will soon face him (Ordinary World). His scheming and embittered uncle Scar lures Simba into a gorge and stirs up a wildebeest stampede, which results in the death of Simba's father, Mufasa (Call to Adventure). Simba escapes to another part of the jungle, leaving Scar to rule the Pride Lands. When, as an adult, he is approached by his childhood sweetheart, Nala, and asked to return and take his place as king, Simba refuses, believing he caused his father's death (Refusal of the Call). Rafiki arrives and persuades Simba to return to the Pride Lands, aided by the appearance of the ghost of Mufasa (Meeting with the Mentor).

Once back at Pride Rock, Simba is horrified to see the condition of the Pride Lands under Scar's monarchy (Crossing the First Threshold). His friends Timon and Pumbaa create a diversion, allowing Simba and Nala to sneak past the hyenas guarding Pride Rock (Tests, Allies, Enemies) where Simba sees his mother Sarabi struck by Scar for criticizing him. Outraged, Simba announces his return. In response, Scar tells the pride that Simba was responsible for Mufasa's death and corners Simba at the edge of Pride Rock (Approach).

As Simba dangles over the edge of Pride Rock, Scar proudly but quietly reveals to Simba that he killed Mufasa. Enraged, Simba leaps up and pins Scar to the ground, forcing him to admit the truth to the pride. A raging battle then ensues between the hyenas and the lionesses (Ordeal).

The lions win the battle, and Simba corners Scar and forces him into exile (Reward). Simba is installed to his rightful place as king of the Pride Lands (Return to the Ordinary World), but Scar only pretends to leave and turns to attack Simba, resulting in a final duel which is ultimately won by Simba (Resurrection Hero). The film concludes with the Pride Lands turning green with life again and Rafiki presenting Simba and Nala's newborn cub as the heir to the throne (Return with Elixir).

We could unpack nearly every Disney film made since 1989 and find the same mythic structure. Vogler's genius was in noting that this story resonates so deeply with audiences that they will take it any way they can get it. In the 1992 book that resulted from his memo, he exegetes films as diverse as *Mad Max* and *Four Weddings and a Funeral*, finding the same essential structure to their storylines. Of course, the mono-myth idea applies to all movies, and so Vogler would have a field day with more obviously adventurous films like the Lord of the Rings and the Matrix trilogies, *Titanic*, *Avatar*, and the recent crop of superhero films like the Spider-Man and Batman series. In fact, in identifying the structure of myth, Joseph Campbell captured the desires in the human heart to which all great stories refer—the desire for redemption, being part of something greater, good ultimately triumphing against evil, and so forth.

What Did Jesus Do?

Our point isn't to make an examination of popular film but to illustrate that the yearning for a heroic adventure lies just beneath the surface of our consciousness; film, television, literature, sports, and travel are in a sense vicarious adventures. But because they are vicarious adventures, we can live them out through the lives and stories on the screen. They can act as inoculations against the real adventure virus that we need to expose ourselves to.

If Campbell and Vogler are right—and what they have articulated resonates well with our most primal and elemental story—we should pay close attention to it. It tells us something important about all human yearning. Note the remarkable parallels between Campbell's heroic journey and the story of Paul; the calling of Moses; the vocations of Isaiah, Jeremiah, or the Twelve, for that matter.

But when it comes to Jesus, you can pretty much check off each of Campbell's stages against the Gospel narratives of Matthew, Mark, or Luke. Interestingly, it's as though the gospel story of Jesus is the archetypal heroic journey, the embodiment of the very adventure that all people in every epoch have desired. Consider the following table that can be used to outline the story of Jesus as the Hero's journey.

Stages	Vogler/Campbell	Gospel
Ordinary World	The hero's normal world before the story begins.	We meet Jesus growing up in obscurity in the ordinary town of Nazareth, and eventually working as a carpenter.
Call to Adventure	The hero is presented with a problem, challenge, or adventure.	Jesus is increasingly aware of his calling but awaits the appointed hour to commence his public ministry.
Refusal of the Call	The hero refuses the challenge or journey, usually because he's scared.	Well, maybe there's no correlation here, but as a man he does obediently submit himself to the will of God.
Meeting with the Mentor	The hero meets a mentor to gain advice or training for the adventure.	Jesus presents himself to his cousin, his forerunner, John the Baptist to be baptized into his messianic role.
Crossing the First Threshold	The hero leaves the Ordinary World and goes into the Special World.	Jesus retreats to the wilderness for a period of spiritual preparation for his public ministry where he is tested severely by the devil.
Tests, Allies, Enemies	The hero faces tests, meets allies, confronts enemies, and learns the rules of the Special World.	Jesus faces various tests; he calls twelve disciples; he confronts enemies and teaches the lessons of the kingdom of God.
Approach	The hero has hit setbacks during tests and may need to try a new idea.	Jesus is betrayed, arrested, tried, and tortured by his enemies before being rejected by the crowds and condemned to die.
Ordeal	The biggest life-or-death crisis.	Jesus suffers and dies to make a way for human beings to be reconciled to the Father.
Reward	The hero has survived death, overcomes his fear, and now earns the reward.	Jesus defeats death and rises to life three days later, his resurrection guaranteeing the salvation of all those who repent.
The Road Back	The hero must return to the Ordinary World.	Jesus returns to his friends, including those who betrayed him, to invite them to join his mission in extending the kingdom of grace around the world and throughout history.
Resurrection Hero	Another test where the hero faces death—he has to use everything he's learned.	Jesus promises his followers he will be with them to the end of the age and commissions all future followers to go forth and make disciples.
Return with the Elixir	The hero returns from the journey with the "elixir," and uses it to help everyone in the Ordinary World.	Jesus the Hero promises to return to regenerate all things and build a new heaven and a new earth.

The correlation between Campbell's elemental story and the story of the Gospels tells us that Jesus is actually the object of all human yearning. We want him, we want to live like him, we want to know him. His is the story in the hearts of all true storytellers. When telling heroic stories about Jedi knights or samurai warriors, Viking invaders or Texan sheriffs, Zion versus Babylon in the Matrix series, or the redemption of cynical, wounded warriors in *Avatar*, storytellers are inadvertently retelling the Jesus story, albeit partly or inaccurately.

Myth-Making

So much for the structure of myth, what about the meaning of myth? Why is it so important, and why does it seem to have such a potent hold on the human imagination and such direct access to the human heart? Hopefully when we grasp this, we will understand the potency of story, adventure, and our sense of involvement in the unfolding of events. Here we must turn to that great re-mythologizer of gospel truths, C. S. Lewis, for help. But first we must understand what we mean by *myth* here: It is "the dramatization in temporal terms of things seen from the non-temporal standpoint of eternity. . . . A myth is not about something that once happened, but rather about something that is *always* happening; the narration of a divine event."[4] Myth is therefore not just a story; it is the Story beyond the story, and it is the realm in which people most live. And because it appeals to the depths of human longing and search, it acts as a kind of master key to the soul—we can use it on what door we like. Listen to C. S. Lewis:

> The value of the myth is that it takes all the things we know and restores to them the rich significance which has been hidden by the "veil of familiarity." The child enjoys his cold meats (otherwise dull to him) by pretending it is a buffalo, just killed with his own bow and arrow. And the child is wise. The real meat comes back to him more savory for having been dipped in a story: you might say that only then is it the real meat. If you are tired of the old real landscape, look at it in a mirror. By putting bread, gold, horse, apple, or the very roads into a myth, [Lewis is here talking of Tolkien's Lord of the Rings] we do not retreat from reality, we rediscover it. And as long as the story lingers in our mind, the real things are more themselves.[5]

Speaking of Tolkien's Lord of the Rings, Lewis says that the myth of Sauron teaches us that evil is real and enduring; that the war of the Ring is only one of a thousand wars against him. Every time we shall be wise to fear his ultimate victory, after which there will be "no more songs." "Every time we win we shall know that our victory is impermanent."[6] If we insist on having a moral of the story, that is it: a recall "to that hard, yet not quite desperate insight into Man's unchanging predicament by which heroic ages have lived."[7]

Lewis says elsewhere that

> if we take the imagery of Scripture seriously, if we believe that God will one day give us the Morning Star and cause us to put on the splendor of the sun, then . . . both the ancient myths and the modern poetry, so false as history, may be very near the truth as prophecy. . . . We cannot mingle with the splendors we see. But all the leaves of the New Testament are rustling with the rumor that it will not always be so.[8]

And the wonderful thing is that for us as Christians, we can draw deeply from the wells of longing for redemption that is part of the structure of myth. C. S. Lewis also suggested that all people harbor desires they cannot name, memories of a home they have lost, traces of a story they love but have forgotten. In his essay "The Weight of Glory," he writes, "We cannot tell it because it is a desire for something that has never actually appeared in our experience. We cannot hide it because our experience is constantly suggesting it, and we betray ourselves like lovers at the mention of a name."[9]

This desire, he said, is precisely for the glory that Jesus has promised, and every whisper or trace of that glory sets off our desire for it once again. Of course, our understanding of what it means remains inchoate and symbolic, for we cannot grasp it, yet the thing we desire is real, and we have been made to find our fulfillment in it. We would suggest, following Lewis, that the reason the hero's journey has appealed to so many throughout history and continues to bedazzle its hearers to this day, is because it piques our desire for the glory of Jesus. Lewis said, "For they [our yearnings] are not the thing itself; they are only the scent of a flower we have not found, the echo of a tune we have not heard, news from a country we have not visited."[10]

Why explore this material on myth-making here? Well, we think it vital to touch base with it because it clearly has a significance in and helps us understand human longing and therefore human motivation. It also gives us insight into the mythic appeal and nature of the gospel as adventure, because the very concept of the incarnation and the *missio Dei* are in some way basic to all myths that incorporate adventure at the center of the story. Again it was Lewis who noted,

> As myth transcends thought, Incarnation transcends myth. The heart of Christianity is a myth which is also a fact. The old myth of the Dying God, *without ceasing to be myth* comes down from the heaven of legend and imagination to the earth of history. It *happens*—at a particular date, in a particular place followed by definable historical consequences. . . . By becoming fact it does not cease to be myth: that is the miracle.[11]

Campbell's hero story resonates because it is like news from another country. In this respect we would suggest that our love of extreme sports, our quest for adventure, our desire for heroic novels and films, all play into this same yearning. They are the echoes of an unheard tune—the story of Jesus. The quest for heroic adventure then is a quest for the gospel, although it might not be seen that way by everyone. And so, when churches distance themselves from such adventure, they are inhibiting a fundamental human impulse and desire to be part of something significant that has eternal consequences.

Reel Communitas

Hollywood knows how to reach into human hearts, and we can take a page from their book in trying to renovate our message and our churches through the power of the gospel. What better way to illustrate the power of liminality-communitas than to explore their mythic re-presentation in the form of movies?

For instance, as referenced earlier, liminality-communitas was powerfully captured in Peter Jackson's epic movie of Tolkien's Lord of the Rings trilogy. This story has all the hallmarks of our greatest mythic portrayals of adventure. Against all odds, and up against the most evil of foes, the most unlikely group is forged into the

Fellowship of the Ring that together saves the day and changes the course of history.

In the third installment, *The Return of the King*, there is a charming scene where, after Frodo and Sam have finally destroyed the ring and Mordor has been defeated, the four hobbits return to normal life in sleepy Hobbiton. There, they find themselves at a large wooden table at a noisy, busy inn. The other drinkers are laughing and carousing, going on with life as they had always known it. But Frodo and his friends have experienced an adventure like no other. They have looked death in the face many times, and by rallying together they have not only survived but triumphed over evil. What of this experience could their friends and neighbors possibly understand? As they raise their tankards of ale to their lips, they look at each other—a long, knowing look. As their eyes meet, something unspoken is powerfully communicated. They *know* each other. No words can express what they're thinking, but they know each other's thoughts. This is the society found only in communitas.

The Lord of the Rings trilogy are not the only films that celebrate communitas. It appears that the majority of movies have a liminality-communitas dialectic at their core. So many, in fact, that we suggest their popularity tells us something about the deep yearning for communitas we all share. We love watching films in which a band of friends find deeper connection through the challenges thrown at them by an external threat, precisely because we desire that same connection with our own friends. War movies like *Saving Private Ryan*, *Blackhawk Down*, and the mini-series *Band of Brothers* work because, not only do they attempt to depict war accurately, they focus on the intensity of the relationships forged between soldiers in combat. In *Saving Private Ryan*, the band of soldiers are stunned to learn that their captain (played by Tom Hanks) is in fact a schoolteacher in civilian life. In the liminal experience of war, he has been changed, enlarged, by the ordeal of leadership.

In buddy movies like *Boys on the Side*, *Thelma and Louise*, and *Oceans 11* (*12* and *13*), the characters undertake a challenge and develop ever-deeper intimacy as the story unfolds. The same can be said for the Matrix trilogy and *O Brother, Where Art Thou?*

Even more powerful (and common) are those films where characters who are opposites are thrown together. In *Rain Man*, a selfish, immature young man (Tom Cruise) is forced to drive his autistic older brother (Dustin Hoffman) across America to retrieve his inheritance. By the end of the journey, Cruise's character has been transformed by the relationship he has developed with his brother. In the cult classic *The Princess Bride*, an unlikely band of adventurers (a pirate, a vengeful Spaniard, a giant, and a princess-to-be) are bound together in their attempt to overthrow an evil prince. A similarly unlikely bunch come together to build a baseball diamond in a cornfield in *Field of Dreams*. And, of course, just about every *Mighty Ducks*–style sports film capitalizes on our desire to see a ragtag bunch of also-rans transformed into a force greater than the sum of the individual parts. And the daddy of all road movies, *The Wizard of Oz*, describes a liminal journey in which each character literally contributes a different part to the body as a whole—the Scarecrow's brain, the Tin Man's heart, the Lion's courage, and Dorothy's sense of destiny.

The hunger for community is a legitimate one, but to pursue it for its own sake is a mistake. When we seek to build community without the experience of liminality, all we end up with is the kind of pseudo-community that pervades many churches. It's more like a support group than a communitas. In David Fincher's incendiary film *Fight Club*, the main character/narrator, played by Edward Norton, is lost in a quagmire of materialism and meaninglessness. He has an odious job as a recall coordinator for a major automobile company and tries to fill the void in his life by buying new furnishings and appliances for his IKEA-inspired home. The pain is too great, though, leading to a numbing cycle of sleepless nights and pointless days. When he tries to get some prescription drugs for his insomnia, his doctor refuses, unsympathetically comparing his psychological "pain" with the real physical pain experienced by victims of testicular cancer. In reaction, Norton's character attends a support group for cancer sufferers and soon finds himself becoming addicted to a variety of support groups. For the first time in his life, he gets in touch with his emotions and cries freely. However, Marla Singer (Helena Bonham Carter), another tourist in the land of genuine suffering, spoils this therapeutic release for him by holding up a mirror to his dishonesty.

Norton's character wants the kind of community he can find at a support group. And for a time it is helpful, but it has its limits. He can never fully realize the kind of communion he desires because he is not on the same threshold as the other members of the group. He and Marla don't actually have cancer or alcoholism. They can look like sufferers, faking it for a period, but ultimately the ordeal of cancer is not one they can share. For communitas to develop, the members of a group must all be involved in the same challenge. In Terence Malik's war film *The Thin Red Line*, Tony Shalhoub plays a captain who refuses to order his men over a ridge, knowing that it is securely held by well-armed Japanese forces. Despite several orders from above he steadfastly refuses to give the word to charge the hill. Later, when he is relieved of his duty, he talks to his men declaring that they are like his sons. They gather around to bid him farewell, knowing he has shared their ordeal and saved them from certain death. This scene can be juxtaposed with a later one, where, after the campaign has ended, the new captain (George Clooney), who has never seen action, gives the men a speech in which he says they should look at him as if he were their father. Shalhoub's speech is heartfelt and moving. Clooney's is shallow and ridiculous.

Building community for its own sake is like attending a cancer support group without having cancer. It's like asking soldiers you haven't fought with to imagine you are their father. And it's like a church demanding allegiance and weekly attendance without linking its attenders with a cause to which they can give their lives. It's no different from the church holding endless Bible study groups or supplying countless sermons for the purpose of learning information that will rarely be utilized. Have you ever noticed how many men will attend church occasionally and begrudgingly, but when there is a church working bee, they'll turn up joyfully and work hard all day?

Working bees create a mini-communitas. So do short-term mission trips and youth mission trips. So does church planting. But simply attending weekly church services does not. It's like sitting at the apostles' feet and drinking in their teaching in Jerusalem in the first century. It might serve some purpose, we suppose. But the ultimate purpose of the Jerusalem church was to go and make disciples of all nations. There's no question that the apostles' teaching was essential, but not as an end in itself. Their teaching was meant to mobilize ordinary believers to go into the world, baptizing new disciples and teaching them all that Christ commanded them. As mentioned earlier, it wasn't until persecution drove the first Christians out of Jerusalem that they discovered their purpose, and that purpose threw them together into a liminal state, as a missionary movement.

Attending a respectable, middle-class church in a respectable, middle-class neighborhood is not usually a liminal experience. Joining a peace movement in a nation obsessed with military might is. Traveling to Indonesia to help with the international relief effort after a tsunami is. Joining a church planting team is. Why do our churches often miss this experience of communitas? For no other reason than that they often avoid liminality, opting for a safer, more secure environment.

We're not for a minute suggesting that Christian communitas shouldn't cater to the need we all have for safety. Indeed they should. But we must fashion safe spaces not as alternatives to missional engagement in our world, but as parallel experiences to that engagement. Whenever we have led or been part of a missions team, we have ensured that there are protocols for those who are tired, emotionally depleted, or spiritually dry to retreat and be replenished. But this hasn't stopped the mission from continuing. It happens parallel to the ongoing purpose of the team. Rather than seeing the safety of community as the end result of someone else's adventure, we need to see it more like a way station on the side of the road—a much-needed rest for the journey ahead. This much we can be sure of: we have not yet arrived, there is still a lot of work to be done, and our King is coming.

You Are a Hero, Now Be One

As we have seen, mission is the church's primary form of adventure, or at least the catalyst of it. By allowing the great divorce between church and mission, we are selling people short. We don't do people any favors by protecting them from the adventure of a missional journey. One of two things usually happens when we restrain our people from diving into adventure. Either they abandon the Christian adventure in search of something seemingly more exciting, or they launch out into a solo experience of mission. But when we factor the adventure of mission into the equation, then everything the church does is somehow connected to, or catalyzed by, mission, including discipleship. We raise young men and women to embrace the missional vocation as a distinct and inseparable part of their identity as a Jesus follower. They are missionaries, embarking on the missionary's journey right from the start.

Can you imagine how exciting it would be for young Christians if they understood their vocation as disciples as not dissimilar from the hero's journey—including a call to adventure, the role of mentors and friends and allies, and the importance of trials and ordeals? Overcoming for the cause? Currently, young Christians reach adulthood bored with their church experience, and with little or no sense of their calling as missionaries. They have been taught the Bible since they were little, but they have so little use for the information they have been given that it goes in one ear and out the other.

What would happen if we saw ourselves as embarking on an incredible adventure together, and if the learning we received was pertinent to the very ordeal we were undertaking? It's not unlike those safety announcements you get on every airplane flight you take—you seriously don't think you're going to have to ditch into the Atlantic or make a miraculous landing on the Hudson River, so you pay no attention to them. Compare your attitude toward safety announcements on commercial airlines to the instruction you receive when going skydiving for the first time. You pay the utmost attention to those skydiving instructions. It's a matter of life or death!

We have a friend who says she believes churches should get Bible teaching "on a need-to-know basis." In other words, a church should open their Bibles together and learn from Scripture according to the contextual challenges and ordeals they are currently facing together. Sadly, many Christians don't "need to know" what they hear each Sunday, and so they retain very little of it. Preachers end up feeling like neglected flight stewards being ignored by their complacent passengers throughout the safety announcement.

Now, we recognize believers should have a clear, consistent biblical worldview, and we can't offer Bible teaching based only on felt needs and areas of immediate interest. But frankly, we'd rather teach missionaries, disciples who are hungry for Bible teaching to sustain, enrich, and guide them in the missional ordeal, than churchgoers who have little motivation for hearing the truth. And remember, unused truth is lost truth. It doesn't matter how true we believe the Bible to be, or how effective and gifted our teachers might be. If our congregations are not engaged missionally in the ongoing work of serving the poor, feeding the hungry, challenging society, preaching the gospel, and responding to unbelief, they will have little need for our teaching.

Returning to Paul's ministry, we see what it looks like when mission organizes the discipleship function of a church. Paul had nothing but praise for his beloved Thessalonians, about whom he said,

> We always thank God for all of you, mentioning you in our prayers. We continually remember before our God and Father your work produced by faith, your labor prompted by love, and your endurance inspired by hope in our Lord Jesus Christ. For we know, brothers loved by God, that he has chosen you, because our gospel came to you not simply with words, but also with power, with the Holy Spirit and with deep conviction. You know how we lived among you for your sake. (1 Thess. 1:2–5)

Here he mentions the Thessalonians' faith, love, and hope. They seemed to understand what the Corinthians had yet to grasp (and so Paul spells it out for them, and us, in 1 Corinthians 13). He also marvels at the Spirit's work in their midst and their deep sense of conviction about the truth of the gospel. This is praise any church today would appreciate, but Paul continues, because the faith of the Thessalonians is demonstrated not only by conviction or spiritual manifestation. It is demonstrated in their missional vocation:

> You became imitators of us and of the Lord; in spite of severe suffering, you welcomed the message with the joy given by the Holy Spirit. And so you became a model to all the believers in Macedonia and Achaia. The Lord's message rang out from you not only in Macedonia and Achaia—your faith in God has become known everywhere. Therefore we do not need to say anything about it, for they themselves report what kind of reception you gave us. They tell how you turned to God from idols to serve the living and true God. (1 Thess. 1:6–9)

Paul sees a direct link between faith and missional action. We suspect this might have been informed by his own experience. At the very point of his conversion on the road to Damascus, he is commissioned an apostle to the Gentiles. Paul reports this several times. Conversion and commissioning are interlinked for him, and it seems he cannot imagine faith without calling.

The Thessalonians are models to all believers in that region of the world at that time because their faith produced missional muscle. They turned from idols to the true and living God, and then in spite of persecution they turned resolutely to their calling as missionaries. In so doing they joined a viral church planting movement with one communitas after another taking the gospel to all of Asia, as it was then known.

When mission catalyzes discipleship, new believers should be commissioned as missionaries and mentored by mature missionaries, not merely to learn the names of all the books in the Bible in order, but to discern God's greater calling in their lives and to knit this calling to their conversion to Christ. Too many believers have experienced the great divorce we spoke of earlier. Being converted and being called to mission are seen as two separate experiences, the latter being entirely optional and only for the stout-hearted.

Broadening It All Out

So far, our discussion of the heroic paradigm could give the impression that we are calling people to discover their own personal, individualistic quest, like Frodo. But the challenge of risky adventure is invariably a communal challenge. It is a band of fellow travelers thrown together to engage a greater cause than one of their number could undertake. We need to broaden Campbell's hero myth to include, or more accurately, to *presuppose*, a collective rather than an individual.

Also, one of the most common complaints we have received about our thoughts on liminal church is that people can't imagine living their lives in a constant state of heightened missional activity. Surely, they ask, there must be time for contemplation, regeneration, worship, and time alone with God. Nowhere do we suggest otherwise. As we began, mission must be seen as *one* of the four primary functions of the church, together with discipleship, worship, and community. And as we said from the outset, mission is a marvelous catalyst, or *organizer*, of those other functions, but it must not be undertaken to the exclusion of them.

A way to make this clearer is found in the book *Metavista*, written by two friends of ours, Colin Greene and Martin Robinson. In it they present what they call the "missional matrix," an interactive framework for understanding how a community organized by mission could be shaped without compromising the essential biblical nature of the church. This framework also helps to make sense of the idea of collective heroism. They identify five broad elements to healthy missional activity: leadership, discipleship, mobilization, societal engagement, and communitas. And they see these elements being undertaken within four dimensions. We reproduce it with slight developments here:[12]

Figure 4.1

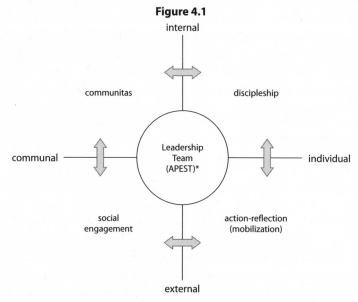

A Missional Matrix[13]
*Apostle, Prophet, Evangelist, Shepherd, Teacher (Eph. 4)

The Missional Matrix

According to Greene and Robinson, the Christian is responsible to serve and strengthen the *internal* life of the church, as well as being involved in the mission, or *external* dimension, of the church. While we are called to be active and reliable members of the *community* of believers, we are also loved by God as *individuals*, and our individuality is never subsumed into the corporate. The church is not an all-assimilating collective like a beehive; it is made of unique individuals bearing the unique stamp of the *imago Dei*. This is seen in Jesus's delightful stories of the one lost coin, the one lost sheep, and the one lost brother (Luke 15). When we discuss the power and importance of communitas, we do so knowing that it must be seen as one of the dimensions of the church's life and mission. Alan developed this idea in his model of a missional DNA in *The Forgotten Ways*, where he highlighted communitas as one of the essential features of a missional community.

With these four dimensions in mind, Greene and Robinson then develop four quadrants in which the missional life of a church unfolds. They are the internal-individual, the external-individual, the external-community, and the internal-community. In each of these quadrants, a different aspect of missional life is catalyzed. It should also be borne in mind that each of the quadrants informs and inspires the others in some measure as well (indicated by the double-headed arrows in the diagram above). By examining each of these quadrants, we can show that while communitas is essential, it sits within a broader matrix of missional activity.

1. The Internal–Individual Quadrant—Discipleship

The church is responsible to create and mature individual disciples, and this is an "internal" aspect of the church, although as we stated earlier, engagement in mission is a marvelous catalyst for discipling believers. Greene and Robinson indicate this in their diagram by showing how the mobilizing of believers into mission helps shape them as disciples. Unless the church is equipping believers to embrace the values and vision of the kingdom of God and turn away from the materialism, consumerism, greed, and power of the present age, it not only abandons its biblical mandate, it is rendered missionally ineffective. Greene and Robinson identify two particular aspects of disciple-making: developing habits of the heart, and embracing spiritual disciplines. On the former they say, "The phrase *habits of the*

123

heart is used to describe those core disciplines which are normally built deeply into the lives of individuals and communities and enable those individuals and communities to flourish."[14]

Following Robert Bellah, from whom they borrow the phrase, they identify important habits of the heart as including an orientation toward community rather than rampant individualism, an abandonment of consumerism, and a separation of happiness from virtue. From the platform of these transformative habits of the heart, the authors then suggest we build a number of spiritual disciplines and undergird a deepening and developing commitment to discipleship. They point out,

> Spiritual disciplines offer us a range of commitments and rhythms which build on other good habits, further reinforcing them but also moving us closer to a capacity to hear God and so develop a sense of direction in relation to our calling or vocation in the world.[15]

This is nothing we haven't written ourselves in such books as *Untamed* (Alan) and *Exiles* (Michael), but it does very helpfully place the exercise of spiritual disciplines within the broader matrix of missional engagement. In our opinion, most people write about spiritual disciplines as though they are ends in themselves, or at least divorced from the liminality of adventurous discipleship. For instance, we have never seen risk-taking, or even mission, suggested as a spiritual exercise. But seeing them as one quadrant, necessarily catalyzed by missional mobilization and in the context of communitas, is very helpful. This takes us back to the Celts' cell and coracle that we mentioned earlier. They are not mutually exclusive experiences. Indeed, each is diminished markedly by the absence of the other.

2. The External-Individual Quadrant—Mobilization

When individual believers are adequately discipled—taught, mentored, corrected, encouraged—they cannot but live out their deep devotion to Jesus in their homes, their workplaces, and their leisure pursuits. This is the external-individual aspect of mission, the mobilization of disciples into the world. Indeed, this is the very place that such discipleship is to be lived out. As David Bosch says,

Discipleship is determined by the relation to Christ himself, not by mere conformity to impersonal commands. The context of this is not in the classroom (where "teaching" normally takes place), or even in the church, but in the world.[16]

Every believer who takes seriously their vocation as a disciple of Jesus will see themselves as a "sent one" wherever they find themselves, and will look to be mobilized into action in that place. As Greene and Robinson make clear,

> There comes a time when as individuals we accept responsibility for the calling we have been given and begin to experiment with a specific ministry to serve others. Every Christian has a vocation that needs to be exercised.[17]

This could take the form of being a "good witness" at work or a good neighbor to those who live nearby, or it could involve volunteering to serve on the PTA or the local neighborhood watch committee. These are the kinds of things individual Christians involve themselves in as an expression of their devotion to Jesus. But there are also those communal missional projects where we are encouraged to join with other believers in a concerted effort for the sake of the gospel. This leads us to the third quadrant.

3. The External-Community Quadrant— Societal Engagement

Greene and Robinson's third quadrant sees believers joining together in a missional project, or a "societal engagement," to use their expression. While affirming the importance of being a strong Christian example in our workplaces, they also point out that it is necessary and important for us to find opportunities to work together as disciples on a joint project. They explain,

> The mobilization of many individuals requires a social context in which the ministries that mobilization produces can be exercised. Most Christians will engage with the world within a relatively small distance from their home and workplace. Of course, for some people the workplace can be a huge distance from the home and that raises particular challenges for those individuals—but again, most people

wish for some kind of engagement with the community of people where they worship, where they have friends, where their children go to school, and where they play sport or socialize with others.[18]

This external-community quadrant is essential for healthy mission, and we would argue, for healthy discipleship. Many people have told us that they see their primary "calling" is to serve the church and to simply be a good witness at work and in their neighborhood. They have no need, nor desire, to join a communal missional project. But when this quadrant is missing, so is the opportunity for communitas, and indeed, so is the opportunity for healthy discipleship. There is something insidious about the idea of solo discipleship. As we mentioned earlier, Paul's letters were written to communities, and they presuppose a communal response to the teaching they contain. We don't dismiss the validity and importance of individual witness, but we can't step away from the biblical imperative of communal mission.

4. The Internal-Community Quadrant—Communitas

When disciples adopt a communal missional project, they find that the internal-community dynamic is that of communitas. As we've been saying, the communal aspect of the church-in-mission is that deep, intimate sense of comradeship Victor Turner termed *communitas*. We don't intend to say much more here, other than to point out its relation to discipleship and engagement. According to Greene and Robinson's missional matrix, you can't expect to experience communitas unless you are engaged in mission with fellow disciples.

Having looked briefly at these four quadrants, it might be tempting to see them in some simplistic cause-and-effect relationship—when we disciple individuals, they will naturally be mobilized into action, and when enough of them are so mobilized, they will get involved in joint projects, and that in turn leads to communitas. It might be illustrated like this:

Figure 4.2

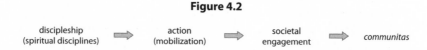

discipleship (spiritual disciplines) ⇒ action (mobilization) ⇒ societal engagement ⇒ *communitas*

By developing their model as a matrix, Greene and Robinson are indicating that there is no linear cause-and-effect at work here. It's not as simple as assuming that if we disciple believers effectively, they will end up being mobilized into service. There are too many incidents of well-trained and discipled Christians never serving anyone. Likewise, it's naive to assume that by just throwing people into a communal missional project, they will automatically experience communitas. Indeed the matrix shows that all four quadrants play on each other quite dramatically. They need to be managed as concurrent priorities, believing that discipleship, personal witness, communal mission, and communitas catalyze and sharpen each other. Combining this with what we believe to be the four functions of the church (more on this later), this can be illustrated as follows:

Figure 4.3

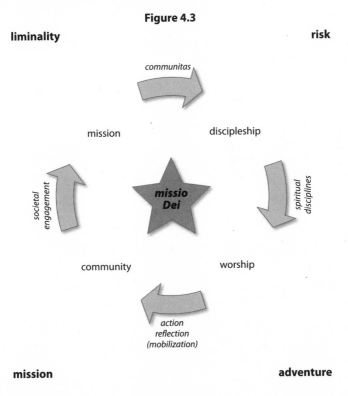

Our growth as disciples influences our personal mobilization and our communal engagement in society. Our communal engagement in society influences our experience of communitas and our growth as disciples. And so on. The missional matrix reminds us that keeping all four quadrants healthy is essential for effective mission. It reminds us that as much as we need to embark upon a heroic journey, we ought rarely to consider doing this alone. Never underestimate the power of a heroic band of brothers and sisters setting out on a risky journey to participate in the unfurling of the kingdom of God in the place where God sends them.

5

Getting Over Risk Aversion

Extracting Truth from Dare

To dare is to lose one's footing momentarily. To not dare is to lose oneself.

—Søren Kierkegaard

You tried your best, and you failed. The lesson is, never try.

—Homer Simpson

It shouldn't be considered remarkable to note that the vast majority of the Bible was written by people facing significant danger and chaos. In fact it is so replete throughout Scripture that any brief list seems inconsequential. The unique history of Israel begins with a single family being called to leave their homeland and journey to a distant and less hospitable place. It features the harrowing individual experiences of the exile Joseph in Egypt and later the servitude of the whole nation under Egypt's oppression. That same history is written by the warrior-adventurer David, the mis-adventurer Job, the absconder Jonah, the expatriate Ruth, the melancholic Jeremiah.

It deals with Israel under threat, under attack, under exile, under condemnation. It features war, oppression, famine, flood, and the rise and fall of empires. And the New Testament is written in the context of the lifestyle of the adventurer-missionaries Paul and Peter and their compatriots. Anchoring all of this is the life of Christ, the persecuted and tormented one. Indeed, very little Scripture is written from the context of stability and security.

This is not to say that there weren't times of relative stability—of course there were times of security and prosperity. But it is a curious fact that in such situations Israel (and church) were (are) not at their best—stability proves to be a far more dangerous experience to the spirituality and faithfulness of God's people. Israel was often at her worst when things seemed to be going swimmingly. And church history proves it is not any different for the new covenant people of God.

In light of this spiritual tendency, Israel is explicitly warned against forgetting the liminal revelations when entering the Promised Land (Deut. 6:10–12 and chaps. 28–32), not only commanding blessings on faithfulness, but curses on the faithlessness that was bound to come through dwelling in the land of promise. Her festivals were profoundly ritualized events that required the people not only to cognitively remember, but also to dynamically participate, in the events that formed Israel—e.g., Passover and Tabernacles recall the deliverance from Egypt and the sojourn in the desert. Once again, liminality plays an important role in developing faithfulness in God's people.

Searching for the Sweet Spot

This constant facing of danger and adapting to the challenges of life is not exclusive to the history of Israel or the founding of the Christian movement. In fact, the idea that all organization, biological and social, emerges from the crucible of chaos is grounded in the very structure of life itself. Chaos theory, the science of how living systems organize and develop, teaches us that

> nature is at its innovative best near the edge of chaos. The edge of chaos is a condition, not a location. It is a permeable, intermediate state through which order and disorder flow, not a finite line of demarcation. Moving to the edge of chaos creates upheaval but not

dissolution; that's why being on the edge is so important. The edge is not the abyss. It's the sweet spot for productive change. And when productive agitation runs high, innovation often thrives and startling breakthroughs can come about. This elusive, much sought after, sweet spot is sometimes called "a burning platform." The living sciences call it the edge of chaos.[1]

The authors of *Surfing the Edge of Chaos* contend that any healthy, growing system needs to move toward the "sweet spot," that zone where the system is under threat and forced to rediscover its inherent logic to move forward. Reflecting on the study of all living systems, they say the more static state of equilibrium or security is actually a precursor to death. "When a living system is in a state of equilibrium, it is less responsive to changes occurring around it. This places it at maximum risk."[2]

It is so counterintuitive for a leader today to push his or her church toward chaos when everything within them tells them to move back to the center, to stability. But this takes us back to Heifetz's understanding about the nature of adaptive leadership. Adaptive leadership moves the system to the edge of chaos—not over, but to the edge of it. Followers want comfort, stability, and solutions from their leaders, but that's babysitting. Real leaders ask hard questions and knock people out of their comfort zones and then manage the resulting distress.[3] The leader's role therefore is to ensure that the system is directly facing up to the issues that confront it, issues that if left unattended, will eventually destroy it. If the organization never seriously faces the problem and stays with it for a reasonable time, it will never feel the need to move to find a genuine and more lasting solution—hence the idea of a "burning platform" mentioned above (and previously in chapter 1). We have long taught the simple formula that it is the role of transformative leadership to sell the problem before trying to evoke a solution. It is only when a church, or any group for that matter, is at this edge of chaos that real innovation takes place.

When Alan reflects back to his early days as the leader of a missional church in Melbourne in the early '90s, he can see all the signs of living systems as proposed here. It was chaotic, fluid, dynamic, and highly missional. In fact, he can see now how that church was forced to go through at least three adaptive leaps during his time with them. Likewise with Michael's current leadership of the missional community "Small Boat Big Sea," which he planted in 2001—that community has also faced the need to make adaptive leaps as it has grown in numbers, as the makeup of its members has changed over time, and as it has been challenged to respond to the needs of its neighborhood. The point is that missional communities are at their very best when they are on the fringes. It is when they settle down and move away from the edge of chaos that things go awry.

By and large, churches are very conservative organizations, and after they have been around just a few years can quickly become somewhat more institutionalized, largely because of the Christendom mode and the assumptions underlying it, but also because of leadership style and influence. On the whole, churches seek to conserve the past, and particularly in the historical denominations their primary orientation is often backward to an idealized past rather than forward to a new vision of the future. As such they are often inflexible institutions that enshrine an inherited tradition. Hence, the mainline churches are leading the decline of the church in the West, due almost entirely to the fact that they are closed systems built squarely on an institutional systems story.

But when liminality, either deliberate or otherwise, is allowed to impact and inform the church, we are propelled outward toward the edge of chaos where it has to constantly adapt to the missional challenge it faces. It becomes the highly responsive learning organization that it should be. The role of leadership here is to continually unsettle the community, holding its feet to the fire of mission and marshalling the God-given potential that emerges in times of dissonance and uncertainty. Part of the key to effectively "surfing the edge of chaos" involves helping community members to overcome the toxic levels of risk aversion currently present in our churches. Because risk aversion is perhaps one of the major killers of adventurous discipleship and mission in the life of the church, it is worth taking a deeper look into it.

The Remarkable Story of Risk

In his great tragedy *Prometheus Bound*, Aeschylus retells the legend of Prometheus, the Greek Titan and brother to Atlas, who stole fire from Zeus to give it to mortals. By sharing with humankind that which belonged only to the gods, he was condemned to suffer eternally by being bound to a rock while a great eagle ate his liver every day only to have it grow back to be eaten again the next day. The moral of the tale is that you shouldn't even think about crossing the dividing line between immortals and mortals.

Borrowing from this idea, philosopher-economist Peter Bernstein penned *Against the Gods: The Remarkable Story of Risk*, in which he argues that the people who mastered the calculation of probabilities, beginning in sixteenth-century Italy, stole from the gods something much more precious than fire. They seized the knowledge of the understanding of risk. Given the current level of risk aversion present in so many churches, it will be helpful to have some insight into the nature and benefits of risk, particularly as it affects the formation of community.

It is Bernstein's contention that by calculating probabilities we do the next best thing to seeing the future: we make intelligent decisions—and take control of our lives—on the basis of scientific forecasts. For Bernstein, the mastery of risk is the foundation of modern life, from insurance to the stock market to engineering, science, and medicine. In fact, he says, the mastery of risk is what divides modern from ancient times. The ancient Greeks, for example, adept as they were with numbers, regarded mathematics as belonging to the higher realm of intellectual pursuit, not the messiness of daily life. Amazingly, Bernstein says of ancient Greek dice-rolling, "Though people played these games with insatiable enthusiasm, no one appears to have sat down to figure the odds."[4] If anyone had, they would have cleaned up.

From the early 1500s there appeared a string of philosophers and mathematicians who did try to clean up, including such giants as Galileo, Pascal, Newton, Gauss, Poincare, von Neumann, and Keynes. Blaise Pascal, for instance, is best remembered as a religious philosopher, but as a callow young mathematician, he teamed up with Pierre de Fermat on a solution to an old conundrum: how to divide the stakes of an uncompleted gambling game. With its implications for prediction in other fields, Bernstein says, Pascal and Fermat's solution became "the cornerstone of modern insurance and other forms of risk management."[5]

In 1738 an interesting paradox in risk assessment came to light, courtesy of the Dutch-Swiss mathematician Daniel Bernoulli. Known as the Petersburg paradox, it suggests a game between two men called Peter and Paul in which Peter tosses a coin continuously until it comes up heads. If it comes up heads on the first toss, Paul wins one ducat and the game is over. If it takes two tosses, Paul wins two ducats. If it takes three tosses, he wins four ducats, and so forth. The question is, how much should Paul be willing to pay to play this game with Peter?

The paradox is this: the standard calculation of expected value indicates that the value of playing the game is infinite. The calculation looks like this:

$$(\tfrac{1}{2} \times 1) + (\tfrac{1}{4} \times 2) + (\tfrac{1}{8} \times 4) \ldots = \tfrac{1}{2} + \tfrac{1}{2} + \tfrac{1}{2} \ldots = \text{infinity}$$

Nevertheless, no ordinary person would be willing to pay more than a few ducats to play this game. Bernoulli's explanation is that our assessment of the value of the winnings decreases as the probability of the winnings gets smaller. Mathematically, the probability of the game going to, say, twenty tosses, is 1/1,048,576, and the payoff is 524,288 ducats. However, although the expected value is still $\tfrac{1}{2}$, the probability is so small that we effectively evaluate it as zero. In our minds, the expected value of the game is not the infinite series above, but a series that stops after ten or twenty terms.

As an experiment, some computer geek wrote a program to play this game a few million times and determine the average payout. It came out to around 10 ducats. He supposed you'd have to play an infinite number of games to get the infinite payoff, which certainly justifies our instinctive reluctance to value the game very highly if we only get to play once.

If all this math sounds a bit intimidating, the bottom line is that Bernoulli's paradox necessarily invites a discussion about the way people rank risks. And for that discussion we need to speed through time from eighteenth-century Europe to twentieth-century America, because it was at Princeton in 1979 that Daniel Kahneman and Amos Tversky proposed Prospect Theory to describe the decisions people make between different risk options based on their perceived probabilities.

In effect, Prospect Theory says that people aren't generally risk averse; they are loss averse. For example, give a group of people the choice of $1000 or a 50 percent chance of winning $2000 and most will choose the sure thing and take the $1000. However, give them a choice of losing $1000 immediately against a 50 percent chance of losing $2000, and most will take the risk. This offers an explanation for the fact that people who invest their life savings very conservatively will simultaneously buy lottery tickets. Apparently, this pattern of being unwilling to accept a sure loss has been verified over and over in a variety of circumstances and confirms something basic about human nature: people behave irrationally even when they know they are doing so.

To illustrate this, Bernstein relates an anecdote about a distinguished Soviet professor of statistics who showed up at an air-raid shelter during a German bombardment. Until then, he had scoffed at the prospect of being hit. What changed his mind? "Look," he explained, "there are 7 million people in Moscow and one elephant. Last night, they got the elephant."[6]

In the American film *Along Came Polly*, writer/director John Hamburg approaches this idea, albeit more ludicrously. The story centers on Reuben Feffer (Ben Stiller), an actuary whose job is to analyze risk for insurance purposes. Naturally, as a risk analyst, he prefers to live his own life in complete safety and free from any unnecessary risk as well. This means that he considers such ordinary activities as salsa dancing or eating spicy Moroccan food to be too risky to undertake. His prized possession is a computer insurance program called the Risk Master, which he uses to measure clients' risk in percentages.

When he meets the chaotic and free-spirited Polly (Jennifer Aniston) his risk-averse life is sent into a tailspin. He is attracted to Polly, but by every measurement he can think of, she is a disaster in terms of risky behavior. He tells her,

> I know that I have a .013 percent chance of being hit by a car on my way home. Or a one in 46,000 chance of falling through a subway grate. So I try to manage that risk by avoiding danger and having a plan and knowing what my next move is. And I guess you don't exactly live your life that way. Yeah, which is great, but I'm not gonna ever be

a dirty dancer, and I don't eat food with my hands, and I really like you, but I just don't think this is gonna work out.[7]

Of course, like all romantic comedies, things do work out for these two, but not before Reuben is forced to confront what would be lost and what gained if he lives his life by the Risk Master and lets the crazy Polly go. In this instance, losing Polly is worse for him than the gains of avoiding her anarchic lifestyle. It's all about Reuben letting go of his need to control everything; it's ultimately love that empowers him to do so.

Some church leaders can be very much like Reuben in this respect. They want to embrace the crazy, anarchic call to mission, but they are more afraid of what would be lost if they did so. Taking up the call to risky, liminal mission might sound appealing to them, but they fear the impact this might have on their congregations. They feel the weight of history on their shoulders and don't want to be known as the pastor who led the congregation into chaos and disintegration. We acknowledge this anxiety, but we remind loss-averse church leaders of what could ultimately be lost if the call to missional adventure is finally rejected or even ameliorated. Missional adventure is like the free-spirited Polly—beautiful, disordered, hectic—and the possibility of losing her should frighten us more than the fears we have of losing members of our congregation, or our position, or the order in our lives. Like Reuben, only love can empower us to overcome our loss aversion.

Addressing Our Loss Aversion

These theories of risk assessment highlight how brilliant Jesus's outlook on life was. He begins with our loss aversion, tackling it head-on from the very outset: "For whoever wants to save his life will lose it, but whoever loses his life for me will find it" (Matt. 16:25). In fact, he repeats this proverbial statement over and over. It is a central theme in his teaching, and in all four Gospels.[8] If we could be freed from our aversion to loss, our whole outlook on risk would change. We would be free indeed. Surely, then, this explains Paul's monumental courage as we observed in the previous chapter.

His attitude to risk—dueling with wizards, debating scholars, staring down rioters—has grown from the fundamental assumption that he has nothing to lose. He has lost his life for Jesus's sake and is truly free from fear. This is why he can dare to say, "May I never boast except in the cross of our Lord Jesus Christ, through which the world has been crucified to me, and I to the world" (Gal. 6:14). And,

> I eagerly expect and hope that I will in no way be ashamed, but will have sufficient courage so that now as always Christ will be exalted in my body, whether by life or by death. For to me, to live is Christ and to die is gain. If I am to go on living in the body, this will mean fruitful labor for me. Yet what shall I choose? I do not know! (Phil. 1:20–22)

Tough choice, whether to live or die, but they both hold attractions for Paul. In calling Christians to embrace the risk and adventure of mission, a starting point is the addressing of our core aversion to loss. We are averse to loss much more than we are attracted by gain. But this was an aversion that Paul had abandoned by the time he wrote to the Philippians. For him it was all gain, because he had lost his life for Jesus's sake. This reminds us once again of Martin Luther King's axiom that the true revolutionary is the person who has nothing to lose. This was undoubtedly Paul's experience, and it appears to be central to our capacity to embrace risk.

In his book *The Myth of a Christian Religion*, Greg Boyd makes the helpful distinction between the pledge of life and the life we pledge. He explains:

> We all make an initial pledge to surrender our life to Christ, but the actual life we pledge to surrender is the life we live each moment after we make our initial pledge. For the only life we have to surrender is the life we live moment-by-moment.[9]

Pledging one's life in some generalized, even grandiose, sense sounds impressive, but the reality as Boyd points out is that the pledge must be embraced and reembraced every moment thereafter. This is the life we pledge, every darn minute of it. This applies to the pledge a police officer or a judge might make. It's not dissimilar to your local doctor taking the Hippocratic Oath. And we've all seen ceremonies where inductees of whatever kind are invited to "Repeat after me: I, say your name, do solemnly swear . . ." But any of these oaths or pledges are only valuable to the degree that they are lived out day by day. Boyd illustrates his point using his marriage vows as an example. Referring to the promises he made to his wife nearly thirty years earlier, he says,

> But the actual life I pledged to my wife is the life I have lived each moment since I made that pledge. The quality of my marriage, therefore, isn't decided by whether or not I made a pledge twenty-nine years ago. It's decided by how I live out that pledge *now*.[10]

This is part of the key to understanding why many Christians seem so loss-averse. For many of them their relationship to Jesus is located in the pledge of life, not the life they pledged. Their understanding of the gospel as some magical get-out-of-jail-free card means they are satisfied that their responsibility is simply a once-and-for-all decision made many years ago at an evangelistic rally. But to paraphrase Lesslie Newbigin, the gospel is concerned with the completion of God's purpose in the creation of the world, not—to put it crudely—simply with offering a way of escape for the redeemed soul out of history. It is concerned with the work of God to bring history to its true end, a work to which we are all called to contribute. The loss of one's life for Christ's sake isn't a once-and-for-all choice; it is a daily dying, a constant giving up of one's own interests in the interest of the kingdom. We can't resist quoting Greg Boyd on this subject again:

> We tend to assume that our life is still currently surrendered to Christ because we once-upon-a-time pledged to surrender it to Christ—which is why we tend to live largely secular lives, despite our confession of Christ as Lord. We have *theoretically* surrendered to the Kingdom, but the majority of our *actual life* is lived outside the Kingdom.[11]

When adventure informs our activities and mission organizes the other functions of the church, those other functions are enhanced, not diminished. As we've already pointed out, community is formed more richly and deeply when forged in the crucible of missional activity. But likewise, discipleship—the formation of individuals more and more into the likeness of Christ—occurs with greater effectiveness when organized by liminality and mission. That is because the missional imperative demands that we die each day, that we live the life we pledge for a purpose beyond ourselves.

People resist mission because they are under-discipled, but they are also under-discipled because of the absence of any missional challenge. We seriously question whether Christians today need more teaching and training before being sent into mission. The memberships of most of our churches are full to bursting with Bible teaching. The reason it seems they haven't retained much of it is because they have never had to utilize it in a missional context. We say, take people into mission, confront them with the risk of godly service, and we guarantee they will be desperate for a biblical perspective on life.

The Removal of Risk in Contemporary Society

But there's more to understanding the nature of risk than the exploration of loss aversion. The remarkable story of risk hasn't been fully told until we include some discussion of the sociological dimension. The preeminent sociologist in this field is the Munich-based Ulrich Beck, whose 1986 work *Risk Society* is a standard text on the subject.

Like Bernstein, Beck thinks our current understanding of risk is a distinctly modern phenomenon, but for a different reason. He suggests that the postindustrial society views risk differently than the preindustrial world. In a preindustrial world, the fate of society is shaped by naturally occurring hazards like disease, flood, famine, and the like, along with socially determined hazards such as invasion and conquest, regressive forms of thought and culture, and rigid class structures. But today, our fate is increasingly bound up with risks that are deliberately undertaken—for the sake of benefits conceived in advance—by means of our technological mastery over nature. In other words, the risks we chance today are not assessed by the probability that some force beyond our control might turn against us, but by an assessment of the risks posed by our own technological activity in the world. Beck says,

> In contrast to all earlier epochs (including industrial society), the risk society is characterized essentially by a lack: the impossibility of an external attribution of hazards. In other words, risks depend

on decisions, they are industrially produced and in this sense politically reflexive.[12]

He takes this position so far as to actually define risk as "a systematic way of dealing with hazards and insecurities induced and introduced by modernization itself."[13] In effect, Beck is writing a diatribe against risk management as practiced by so many risk experts, namely, as an exercise in bureaucratic rationality, technocracy, and contempt for the public perception of risk. The English call this kind of bureaucratic risk management the "Nanny State," a society wherein every perceived risk is considered ahead of time, and legal provisions are made to minimize potential harm. Beck's point is that it is the state-based and funded technologies that create the risks in the first place, and then they remove our capacity to assess them by enacting laws restricting them. In other words, there is both the increasing and the removal of risk at the same time: a risk society, to refer to the title of his book.

Rudy Rasmus is the unconventional pastor of St. John's Downtown, a predominantly black church where a third of the members are either homeless or recently homeless. His work at St. John's has been to awaken the spirits of the forgotten people of Houston: the jobless, the impoverished, and the addicted. In an old Methodist church building under a freeway overpass, thousands each week are offered hot showers and nourishing meals. There is an AIDS clinic and a youth center. Every day, the sprawling facilities at St. John's are full of people who suffer from mental illness, drug addictions, and AIDS.

While visiting a large Presbyterian church in the suburbs of Houston, Rudy was surprised to see a plaque on a number of the doors in the children's ministry facility that read, "This is a Peanut Free Room." A peanut-free room? Rudy couldn't figure out why these rich white folks would have peanut-free rooms, and when he asked the minister about this, he was told that many of the kids in that church suffered from allergies to peanuts, so the signs were there to assure parents that their children would be safe from any peanut products.

This was too much for Rudy. He burst into fits of laughter. "In my church, we need gun-free rooms, and syringe-free rooms, and violence-free rooms, but out here in the suburbs their biggest fear is peanuts!!"

This isn't to disregard the very real allergic reactions some children have to the consumption of peanuts, but it does illustrate Beck's point. The greatest fears we hold are often induced by human activity on the environment, and we now have warning signs and legal impediments for the most innocuous, everyday behavior.

In his book *The Barbarian Way*, Erwin McManus recounts the story of his son climbing onto the roof of their home, a stunt that McManus himself admits was the very thing he and his brother would have done when they were young:

> Early one evening, Kim and I were in the front yard when all of a sudden we heard a little voice calling for us from the roof. As soon as Kim saw him her nurturing instinct kicked in and she started commanding him to get back inside. I have to admit I was kind of proud of him right then, but what he did next totally surprised me. Looking past his mom, he asked if he could jump.[14]

Much to Kim's shock, Erwin encouraged his young son to jump off the roof. He continues,

> For Aaron, the jump was fraught with danger. From my vantage point, I could see, though the jump was terrifying, he would find himself triumphant. It was important that he jumped and perhaps even more important that he knew me as the kind of father who would always call him to greater endeavors rather than sending him back to the safe place.[15]

Some readers over a certain age will remember billycart racing, rock fights, tree climbing, jumping off roofs, and other activities almost completely banned these days. Those were the days. Nowadays we raise our children in a cocoon of domesticated security, far from any sense of risk or adventure. And where we ourselves can't reach, the state legislates for safety. Perhaps nowhere is this obsessive risk-averseness more obvious than with those raised in the cotton-woolen safety of the church. They aren't permitted to jump off the roof, or try a cigarette, or smash the windows in a derelict house, so when they reach young adulthood, they fly far from their faith in search of the adventure and excitement that was missing in their childhoods. And yet the bitter irony is that the Christian faith was birthed by men and women with an appetite for risk, and a daring belief in the supreme adventure of Christian mission. Leading young Christians into an even more daring risk than window-smashing or tree-climbing is absolutely essential, and we believe that the liminal adventure of mission is exactly that risk. But it requires godly, compassionate, and strategic leadership.

Many churches are discipling their young people in a hermetically sealed religious environment, attempting to keep the risks of "the world" at bay. It's like keeping tropical fish in an aquarium—so much time and energy goes into keeping the water temperature at the right level, adjusting the Ph levels, cleaning the tank, etc. Used to such an artificial environment, your typical aquarium fish are fragile creatures, completely unable to survive in the ocean. We hate to break it to you, but if you flush the fish from your aquarium down the toilet, they will not end up swimming free on the wild currents of the sea á la *Finding Nemo*. In a sense, when we raise Christian kids in the aquarium-like environment of church culture, we shouldn't be surprised when they so quickly abandon their faith after they leave home or go to college. We think that raising risk-taking missional kids will go a good deal of the way toward preparing them for life in the wide boundless sea.

Leadership and the Risk-Averse

We don't just need fathers who call us to risk and adventure but church leaders who will do so as well. To return to the authors of *Surfing the Edge of Chaos*, we need to remember that equilibrium is death.

Not unlike a short-term mission, where liminality prevails and mission drives the agenda, a church planting team experiences the joy of communitas as well. Most churches start out with dynamic and exciting adventures in evangelism and mission, but like all living things there is movement from the early disequilibrium to a more stable environment of equilibrium. The early days of most churches are unpredictable and wild, but at the same time seem to be filled with a kind of spiritual energy. Why is this the case? What is it about disequilibrium that seems to stimulate life and energy? And what is it about stability that seems to stifle it? Is it because life itself is unpredictable and chaotic, and when we establish organizations that seek to control and minimize the dangers of life, these very organizations actually stifle life? The history of missions is quite clear about this: Christianity is at its very best when it is on the more chaotic fringes.

The assertion that "equilibrium is death" is a derivative of an obscure but important law of cybernetics called the Law of Requisite Variety. This law states that "the survival of any organism depends on its capacity to cultivate (not just tolerate) variety in its internal structure. Failure to do so results in an inability to cope successfully with 'variety' when it is introduced from an external source."[16] To return to our earlier example of tropical fish tanks, the authors give us a great example as to how this law works in reality. They note,

> Fish in a bowl can swim, breed, get food with minimal effort, and remain safe from predators. But, as aquarium owners know, such fish are excruciatingly sensitive to even the slightest disturbances in the fishbowl. On the other hand, fish in the sea have to work much harder to sustain themselves and they are subjected to many threats. But because they cope with more variation, they are more robust when faced with a challenge.[17]

But we know from nature that survival favors heightened adrenaline levels, wariness, and experimentation. Or to put it more succinctly: history favors the brave. This is the reason we previously asserted that the main stimulus for the renewal of Christianity will come from the bottom and from the edge, from the sectors of the Christian world that are on the margins.[18] Following the patterns of all living systems, church history teaches us that movements of adventurous mission in turn generate movements of spiritual renewal in the broader life of the church.

As we've already stated, liminal leadership is the crucial issue here. Leaders are to a social system what a properly shaped lens is to light. A leader focuses the capacities of the organization. Good leaders resist the internal or systemic urge for stability. In fact, they must be prepared to disturb the organization to break the tendency toward equilibrium that threatens to overwhelm it. But this is not achieved quickly, nor without significant wisdom as to human motivations and as to how human communities are activated in a new search for answers. Adaptive leaders must resist the urge to move too quickly or reach for quick fixes or prepackaged solutions. Rather they must activate a corporate search from deep within the ranks of the organization in order to help plot a way forward. This adaptive activation is achieved by

1. Communicating the urgency of the adaptive challenge (i.e., the threat of death or the promise of opportunity);
2. Establishing a broad understanding of the circumstances creating the problem, to clarify why traditional solutions won't work; and
3. Holding the stress in play until "guerrilla" leaders come forward with innovative solutions.[19]

This sequence of activities will obviously generate significant anxiety and tension in the organization, but we had better get used to it if we are going to adapt to the rapidly changing environment of the twenty-first century. One of the skills of adaptive church leadership is to learn to manage the stress and make it a stimulus for innovation in church and mission. The Christian church ought to be highly responsive to its cultural and social contexts. We call this missional muscle, and it is in the constant pursuit of this fitness, or innate adaptability, that the church learns to adjust and respond to the challenges we face in our world. This is definitely part of what it means to be missional: only when the church is truly missional will it become highly sensitive to its environment and develop a natural, inbuilt, and theologically funded mechanism for triggering adaptive responses.

A missional church is therefore a genuine learning organization. It was by being missionally fit that the church in the apostolic and post-apostolic periods not only survived but thrived. They were forced by sheer external conditions to live by their message and adapt to threats as they came along. This made them far more vigorous Christians than their more stable brothers and sisters in more static periods. They did not live in an artificial environment of a churchy fishbowl, but were the ecclesia in all the dangerous spheres of life. And just like our own immune system, what didn't kill them served to make them stronger.

Risk-Taking and the Dangers of Individualism

The other interesting aspect that Ulrich Beck brings to this discussion is how he sees the growth of individualization in society affecting our capacity for risk assessment. He points out that today individuals are freed from any unself-conscious immersion in traditional group decision-making and have to come to terms with their now-unmediated relation to society. Rather than judging the potential of any particular risk as a society or even as a group, we either make these determinations alone or they are made for us by legislators. The end result is that we are developing a society of individuals almost completely unable to measure or embrace risk in a constructive communal fashion. Our legislators tell us that we must wear a seatbelt in our motorcar, that we cannot smoke cigarettes in a restaurant, and that we cannot carry over 100ml of liquid on an airplane. And yet it was human technology that gave us motorcars, cigarettes, airplanes, and explosives in the first place. Our sense of risk is now centrally located around managing the dangers inherent in technology, and our capacity to address them has been taken out of our hands by the state.

Likewise, in churches where a conventional understanding of leadership has prevailed, there is a capitulation to the idea that clergy must act like chief executive officers. The members are rarely consulted, and any missional potential they might hold is simply overlooked. In the end, the clergy think it is their job to make the whole ecclesial machine perform—if they can figure out the best course of action, communicate it down to the troops, and then measure the results, they'll have a high-performance church. But the result is that they often overreach their authority and suppress their people in the process. Which means they end up optimizing their performance within smaller and smaller parameters, so that when the world changes, they have less and less diversity and creativity with which to respond. If only they took New Testament ecclesiology more seriously. Paul assumes that the missional challenges, and their corresponding risks, undertaken by churches will necessarily assume the concerted effort of all the creativity and godliness present within the church. This is why he sees the church as a body, an organism, not an organization.

Those church leaders who embrace the old top-down sergeant-major approach think they're producing tough churches. But they're really producing churches that are less adaptable to change, because they are ignoring the communal missional potential within their church. And they are reinforcing their members' assumption that risk is a bad thing and not for the fainthearted.

And yet, American sociologist Stephen Lyng has illuminated the importance and value of risk-taking behavior, particularly that performed by groups. His concept of *edgework*, described in the book of the same name, is sociology at the edge, the place where norms are renegotiated and boundaries contested. For Lyng and his coauthors, group-based risk-taking (or edgework) is an essential and energizing element of all societies. Or, at least, it should be. Rejecting the usual description of risk-taking activity as frivolous or indulgent, Lyng redeems the idea, seeing *edgework* as a renewing force in our society. He says,

> Risk-taking experience can be understood as either a radical form of escape from the institutional routines of contemporary life . . . or an especially pure expression of the central institutional and cultural imperatives of the emerging social order.[20]

In other words, when we look to our risk-takers we ought to see the shape of things to come rather than a mere rejection of the things that are. He continues:

> Edgework is seen as a means of freeing oneself from social conditions that deaden or deform the human spirit through overwhelming social regulation and control. In the other perspective, edgework valorizes risk-taking propensities and skills in demand throughout the institutional structures of the risk society. Thus, in one view, edgeworkers seek to escape institutional constraints that have become intolerable; in the other, edgeworkers strive to better integrate themselves into the existing institutional environment. These two ways of thinking

about edgework seem mutually exclusive and contradictory, but then again, perhaps they are not. We must at least consider the possibility that people may, on one level, seek a risk-taking experience of personal determination and transcendence in an environment of social overregulation, whereas on another level they employ the human capital created by this experience to navigate the challenges of the risk society. [21]

So, at one level, risk-takers' behavior is instrumental, and at another it is a natural, organic reaction to the institution. Lyng provides a sociological framework for validating the function of risk-takers, for taking notice of their behavior and questioning what it says to us about human nature and about the institution.

But usually, the institution rejects their behavior out of hand, seeing it as having no substantive contribution at all. This reminds us of the mainstream church's reaction to what is now referred to as the emerging church. As numbers of emerging church leaders began to risk with new forms of worship, new approaches to leadership, and, yes, new theological paradigms, the mainstream church reacted with outrage and even fury. Very few conservative mainstream leaders were even willing to countenance the possibility that the emerging church had anything of value to say or any meaningful critique of the existing church worth listening to. It was labeled "liberal" or "reactionary," and we were told it was merely an example of the hypercritical nature of postmodernity. To repeat Stephen Lyng's advice, "We must at least consider the possibility that people may, on one level, seek a risk-taking experience of personal determination and transcendence in an environment of social overregulation."[22] When the church overregulates, there should be no surprise when either risky movements like the emerging church appear, or when individuals abandon the church to embrace the risk of non-institutional Christianity.

More than affirming the role of the risk-takers in society, Lyng reflects on the kind of community they generate precisely because of their collective rebellion. Without actually employing the term *communitas*, he pretty much describes the same phenomenon when referring to group risk taking. He claims that groups organized around risk taking and adventure activities provide a refuge or a pathway or vehicle of expression for those confronting a formal institutional environment that does not fully meet their needs. When society does not allow the freedom or space for adventure and risky enterprises, risk-takers will find community and support with each other in their collective activity.[23] But what would happen if society was prepared to value their behavior and listen to their "message"? What if the comradeship, succor, and support was available within the institution against which they are rebelling? We need leaders in our churches who are able to model a big-hearted, thick-skinned kind of spirituality that doesn't reject the rebels in their midst, but listens, discerns, and validates their legitimate and important perspective. They are given to the church as much as the nurturers and systematizers have been.

After all, the church has everything it needs to get the job done. Nothing has to be imported, for God has provided the very resources it needs to fulfill its distinctive calling, including the risk-takers, the rebels, and the prophets. The trick is to recognize that this capacity, these dormant potentials, are dispersed throughout the body of Christ and not located simply in its leaders. The individualism of our day stymies our capacity for risk, but the New Testament writers knew long ago that no one leader or small group of leaders were to have all the answers. Leadership looks to unleash the missional capacities in *the people of God*. Living systems theory generally teaches us that leaders should disturb, but not direct, their organizations. This means that leaders have to remember that in living systems, things happen that you can't predict, and once they do, those events can set off avalanches with consequences that you could never imagine. You can disturb a church by embracing the risk of taking it into a liminal space and remaining there until the God-given potentials of the people are accessed.

Business guru Richard Pascale and his coauthors suggest three guidelines that will help disturb missional churches: design, don't engineer; discover, don't dictate; decipher, don't presuppose.

1. Design, Don't Engineer

Too much standard church ministry is an attempt to socially engineer certain behaviors or outcomes. It is manipulative and often marginalizes the most creative people in our midst. Instead, leaders should cultivate environments where certain behaviors are stimulated rather than engineer outcomes. In this respect we need to see leadership through the metaphors of the gardener or the midwife rather than that of the CEO or the sergeant-major. Gardeners don't actually produce fruit or flowers. They take seeds, packed full of the latent potential to become a tree or a shrub, and they control the environment to unleash that potential. By tending the garden, watering the plants, adding nutrients, pruning, and protecting, a gardener allows the seed to become what it was created to become. Likewise, a midwife doesn't actually give birth. He or she manages the environment to allow a pregnant woman to successfully birth her child, to bring forth that which she has the innate capacity to deliver.

Missional leadership isn't about social engineering or barking orders to compliant underlings. If there is any manipulation involved, it is about manipulating the environment to unleash the congregation's latent missional potential—its apostolic risk-takers, its prophets, and its pastors.

To illustrate, think about airport gate lounges and the uniform nature of airport etiquette. There is a very obvious, yet unspoken, etiquette in airport lounges. There's no yelling and screaming, even when passengers become frustrated with airline service. No one even talks loudly. There is a quiet order to the environment. But none of this behavior is enforced by signs that say "Don't talk too loudly," "Don't move the chairs," "Don't occupy more than one seat." According to Pascale and his coauthors, those things don't happen due to an invisible hand of design. The environment has been manipulated to elicit certain behavior. The seats are arranged so that people talk to those who are close and they don't shout across the room. The armrests are fixed, so you don't see people sprawling across a couple of chairs. The seats are heavy and bolted down, so you can't pick them up and rearrange them. It looks like it just happens, but the architect has evolved design principles that elicit certain behaviors, without telling people explicitly how to behave.

Factoring liminality, adventure, risk taking, and mission into the church acts like a form of design. By designing them into the ecclesiology itself, we can create an implicit cultural expectation—we can forgo using guilt and heavy-handed rules to coerce the behavior of members. Instead of putting signs up everywhere that say "Take risks, be innovative," adaptive leaders will simply expect that risk taking is part of discipleship and part of the design of the church, and innovation and mission will become a natural and obvious response to the conditions in which the congregation finds itself.

2. Discover, Don't Dictate

Second, as the organization undertakes the challenges set before it, there will be second- and third-order effects—the unpredictable things that need to be addressed but which could never have been anticipated. Their advice to leaders is to adopt a posture of discovery, or of openness to these unfolding challenges. Too many leaders want to dictate the outcomes and force the organization through their predetermined processes. It's important to recognize that leadership can't dictate an outcome. And just as important, once outcomes start to emerge, leaders can't dictate the fastest solution everywhere. This leads to their third maxim.

3. Decipher, Don't Presuppose

As these second- and third-order effects emerge, good adaptive leaders resist their inclination to impose their solutions. Often leaders feel tempted to do so because it feels like the most efficient way of addressing obstacles. But Pascale et al. say that leaders need to recognize there is greater wisdom in the organization itself. How much more can we as Christian leaders acknowledge this in light of Paul's teaching on the giftedness of all believers and the role of the Holy Spirit in the midst of the church? Leaders who want to impose predigested solutions on a church too quickly dampen the inherent wisdom present in the whole community. The trick is to create a design that allows a community to face issues squarely, to learn from itself, to come up with its own solutions to its problems. Or in the case of the church, God's solution mediated by the Holy Spirit through the giftings of the members. Such a process will take longer than the imposition of the leader's solution, but in the long run it will prove to be more efficient, because the wisdom of the collective will be adopted more enthusiastically than that imposed by the leader.

This reminds us of General Electric's well-known Hawthorn Effect. Some years ago, GE did an extensive review of their Hawthorn plant because of its low level of productivity. After a lengthy consultation process with all the workers and management of the plant, the leadership at GE presented a series of recommendations to increase production at Hawthorn. One of these recommendations was to adjust the lighting on the factory floor. The workers had mentioned how the harsh fluorescent lighting made the factory an unpleasant working environment (ironic, given this was a GE plant). After the recommendations were adopted at Hawthorn, productivity went through the roof. It went from being one of the poorest performing plants to one of the most productive. Thrilled with this transformation, GE decided to implement a number of the Hawthorn ideas in other plants, including the replacement of their harsh lights with more ambient lighting. And yet this innovation had little or no effect on productivity in other factories. The Hawthorn Effect tells us that locally developed and owned solutions have far greater effect than those imposed by external experts. The General Electric management had presupposed something of the other factories, based on the experience at Hawthorn.

Similarly, too many church consultants and denominational leaders assume they can distill certain solutions and dictate them to all churches under their influence. Taking the risk of leading a community of believers into mission and then daring to believe that in such a chaotic environment new solutions will emerge from within the community itself is often a step too far for many church leaders. But we are convinced that embracing such a risk is essential. If we can embrace the adventure and risk and equip our churches to lay down their lives and abandon their inherent loss-aversion, who knows what innovation, what freshness, what new insights from the Spirit will emerge. If only we would take the risk!

6

Missional Catalysis

Thinking Differently about the Church and Her Mission

We want to be driven by a purpose that has been tailored just right for our own individual lives . . . when we should be seeing the purpose of all life, including our own, wrapped up in the great mission of God for the whole of creation.

—Christopher Wright

To encounter God is to change.

—Deitrich Bonhoeffer

Austin Stone is a church in Austin, Texas (as its name suggests). It was planted by Matt Carter and Chris Tomlin in 2003 with a vision to reach young adults on the local university campus. Due in part to Tomlin's musical gifts and leadership, the church developed an exuberant spiritual vibe based largely on offering inspiring and challenging worship services for young adults. The church grew phenomenally, reaching around 5,000–5,500 in weekend attendances in only six years! Talk about worship-led revival![1]

Sometime during this period, Matt Carter was diagnosed with cancer, which was surprising for a guy his age and alarming for the young church that he was leading. It was a time for serious spiritual reflection for Matt and the whole team. Matt took extended leave to recover, pray, and seek God for mercy and guidance. While passionately seeking God and his Word, he was constantly confronted with the prophetic passages that called into question the spiritual veracity of worship, particularly when by and large the people were not acting in conformity to God's commands . . . especially in relation to justice and the care for the poor (Isa. 56:1–7; 58:1–14; Jer. 14:12; Micah 6:8; Matt. 15:8). Matt felt that God had utterly nailed him and was asking him to repent and change the church's ways—and this from a church that had built so much on excellent praise and worship.

Returning to work cancer-free, Matt and the team, guided by missional activist Michael Stewart, began to completely revise the focus of their church around mission to the needy people of the city. And because the team had already started to seriously grapple with missional issues, it wasn't hard to win them over. Knowing that God was speaking to them, they began to wholeheartedly put themselves to the task. First up, they had to deal with a massive problem: as is usual for a fast-growing church, they needed a building and had just put in bids for a big piece of property in the suburbs of Austin. The move to the burbs tends to be the way these things usually go—and it suited the demographics: most of those attending were college students, grads, and others drawn mainly from white middle-class backgrounds, and given the spate of marriages and new families, downtown didn't feel quite so natural for them anymore. In what can only be labeled a magnificent act of spiritual courage and leadership, they decided to pass on the move to the suburbs and instead establish themselves as "a church-for-the-city-that-happens-to-meet-on-weekends" in inner-city Austin—in effect they moved into "the hood," with all the associated drugs, crime, poverty, and welfare issues synonymous with many American inner cities.

The property they now inhabit (appropriately called For The City Center) is not a church building but is a community development center built on the idea of sensitivity to the local issues of the people in the neighborhood. This move toward a more consistent missional model of church has meant that they have had to fundamentally rethink their model of ministry and adopt a more fluid movement model. This in turn has meant that they have transitioned their small groups into being missional communities, in effect creating micro-churches organized within a citywide movement still called Austin Stone. Mission is the defining motivation of the movement, and the church continues to explode in new churches, creativity, and conversion. Without doubt, Austin Stone is now one of the leading edge megachurches that has fundamentally redefined itself around being a missional movement in their city.

This story is a good one to start this chapter on because it embodies the very message we want to convey here: that mission must be allowed to once again fundamentally reshape our understanding of church. And why is this the case? Because we believe that somewhere in the nest of paradigms contained in the phrase "missional church" lies nothing less than the future viability of Western Christianity.

One of the great problems we face is the prevailing disconnect between God's mission and God's church. This utterly disastrous divorce must be overcome if we are to advance in our day.

The Great Divorce

As long ago as 1926, the great missiologist Roland Allen was forecasting the tragedy of outsourcing mission from the life of the church:

> We have two organizations for missionary work, one modern, the missionary society, and the other ancient, the Church. But when we consider the organization of the Church today as an organization for missionary work, we must not expect to find it unimpaired in its original purity. In the beginning the Church was a missionary society: it added to its numbers mainly by the life and speech of its members attracting to it those who were outside. Where they went churches were organized, where they settled, men who had never heard of the Church saw the Church, and, being attracted by the life, or by the speech, of its members, learned its secret, joined it, and were welcomed into it. Today members of the Church are scattered all over the world, but they do not carry the Church with them in their own

persons, they were not organized, they very often do not desire the conversion of those among whom they live, they do not welcome them into the Church. So societies are formed to do this for them. The Church, as a Church, is not a missionary society enlarging its borders by multiplying local churches; so societies are formed within it to do its work for it.[2]

Like Allen, we are not casting aspersions on the motivations of the founders of those societies. They were responding to the great need of the world at that time. In the flurry of activity that accompanied the so-called Great Century of mission, foreign mission boards were springing up everywhere, each focused on a certain region of the world, each committed to reaching the world within their lifetime. The nineteenth century was a time of extraordinary expansion in every other field of life. Why not the area of mission as well? But the inadvertent outcome was that it left behind a local church without any real sense of direct involvement in mission and little or no experience of the adventure that it brings. It was the missionaries who became the brave storm troopers of Christianity, slashing their way through jungles, going where no one had gone before. Mission was now reserved for work among the unreached nations and no longer simply happened next door or around the corner. But the churches that had outsourced their missionary activity to the mission societies tended to drift languidly into the role of fund-raiser for the mission societies.

This dilemma was seriously exacerbated when, after World War II, a number of parachurch societies, mainly aimed at reaching young people, were formed. These included Youth for Christ, the Navigators, Campus Crusade for Christ, and so on, and were aimed at reaching students and teens right under the noses of existing churches. Once again, mission was outsourced to specialist agencies, leaving the local church focused primarily around pastoral issues and Sunday worship. Not only did this create the great stepchild, the parachurch, it crippled the church's witness beyond the Sunday gathering. And again, given the significant cultural effect of the postwar baby boom, we understand the historical reasons why such specialization of local mission occurred. But it only deepened the cleft between missionary activity and church activity. Again, long before all this happened, Roland Allen was deeply concerned.

> We may compare the relation of the societies to the Church with the institution of divorce in relation to marriage. Just as divorce was permitted for the hardness of men's hearts because they were unable to observe the divine institution of marriage in its original perfection, so the organization of missionary societies was permitted for the hardness of our hearts, because we had lost the power to appreciate and to use the divine organization of the Church in its simplicity for the purpose for which it was first created.[3]

In the end Allen himself despondently capitulated to this great divorce, concluding that "the divine perfection of the Church as a missionary society cannot be recovered simply by abolishing the missionary societies, and saying, let the Church be her own missionary society."[4]

Maybe not in 1926, but today there is an increasing unease with this "divorce" between mission and church. Allen was ahead of his time. He forecast the situation we now find ourselves in—with *missionless churches* and *churchless missions*, and neither one being all it should be. We contend that the whole missional church conversation was one that the church has been building toward for over a century. And now is the time to have it. A new generation of young Christians is desperate for the adventure of mission. They were raised in the hermetically sealed environment of missionless church, and those who have emerged with their faith still intact are hungry for the risk and ordeal that only true missional activity can offer.

The appetite for adventure and risk is not exclusive to young Christians. In fact, it seems to be a fundamental yearning, knitted into the fabric of the human soul. Where there is no genuine adventure to undertake, we create pseudoadventures of extreme sports: bungee jumping, leaping off skyscrapers, and caving without a torch. Of course, all extreme sports are expressions of our appetite for adventure, but even a game of touch football or beach volleyball is an adventure of sorts, or at least a taste of the real thing.

In missionless churches, there is no adventure. You might get invited to be an usher or to join the church's finance board and perhaps run a Bible study group if you are really good, but there is little by way of genuine communitas, because there is little by way of liminality. It's a simple equation: no liminality, no adventure; no adventure, no mission; no mission, no communitas.

Is a Can Opener a Can Opener . . . ?

As we explain in *The Shaping of Things to Come*,[5] one of the "trick questions" we use to get group discussion going around the idea of purpose is, "Is a can opener a can opener if it can't open cans anymore?" This usually initiates a lively discussion around the idea of essence versus function. When the discussion turns to the application to the idea of church, it generates insight into the issue of purpose of the church. Is the church simply a church because it confesses Christ, or is there some functional test that must be applied? When answering the question, "What do you do with a can opener that doesn't open cans anymore?" most people will say that unless it is fixable, it is not fulfilling that which it was designed for and it should be thrown away.

Without getting too heavy about it, and recognizing that we do live by the grace and love of God, we must recognize that in the Hebraic worldview, fruitfulness and functionality are very important and tend to trump the concept of "essence," which derives largely from Platonic idealism and Greek philosophy. (Idealism basically states that concepts and ideas are real in themselves and are the essence of reality, and forms are just expressions of preexisting ideas.) This is why Jesus always applies the very Hebraic test of fruitfulness to any claims of belief (e.g., Matt. 7:16–20; 12:33; 21:19; Luke 3:8; 13:6–9; John 15; Rev. 2–3). The ultimate test of faithfulness in the Scriptures is not correct intellectual belief (e.g., Matt. 25; Luke 6:46; James 2:12, 21–26) but rather an ethical-functional one—in 1 John it is whether we love or fail in love; in James it is faith with works, about how we care for widows and orphans; in the letters of Peter it is our capacity to suffer in our witness for Jesus; in Hebrews to stay true to the journey. And as politically incorrect as it is to say it, judgment regarding fruitfulness *is* a vital aspect of the revelation of God in the Scriptures (e.g., John 15; Rev. 2–3; as well as the many parables of judgment that lace Jesus's teachings).

It is clear by now that we believe one of the best ways to ensure the church remains true communitas is to constantly factor mission into the equation. Mission provides the church with ongoing liminality, because driven by a holy discontent with the sinful status quo, and expressing the purposes of the kingdom of God, it always impels us to pursue a more faithful, God-soaked future. The church should be shaped by mission because mission has a distinct God-shape to it. We are missional because God is missional. How can God's people be otherwise (Eph. 5:1)? Drawing on the can opener metaphor above, we don't believe that a church is a church if mission is taken out of the equation—or at least it won't be a "church" for long. This is why we are on record claiming that the missional conversation—refactoring mission back into the equation of church—contains the seeds of authenticity and renewal for Christianity in our time and place.

So, here we feel the need to look at how adventure and liminality lead us into a deeper experience of missional Christianity. To do this we will put this conversation about mission-shaped community into its broader context by relating it to the other elemental functions of the church—namely, worship, community, and discipleship.

What on Earth Is the Church For?

We are regularly asked to define what we mean by the phrase *missional church*. Those who ask us are generally looking for a description of a new "model" or a particular style of church. Used to recent innovations like the seeker-sensitive church, the megachurch, the organic church, the emerging church, etc., they assume the missional church must be another such innovation. We get the impression they're looking for a newly minted approach that can be described in a few brief statements. Our standard answer is to say that *a missional church is simply any church that organizes itself around the mission of God in this world*. Because it is about incarnational contextualization in any and every possible culture, it cannot be about a particular style of worship or an innovative model of leadership. It's not even concerned with any particular set of creedal statements. Any church of orthodox biblical beliefs can (and ought to), in theory at least, become missional. So it's certainly possible to imagine a missional Presbyterian church or a missional Baptist church, or for that matter, a missional Arminian church or a missional Calvinist church—or further, a missional emerging church, or a missional house church, or a missional simple church.

The missional church is not a new trend or the latest new technique for reaching postmodern people. It is a way of doing and being church that transcends the particular predilections or preferences of its members. It is a radical challenge to many churches because it is not proposing an "add-on" to what a church might currently do. It is proposing a return to the center, a comprehensive recalibration of the church, a rediscovery of mission as its organizing function. So what does it mean to make mission the organizing function of a church?

The Marks of the Church

Ever since the Reformation, Protestants have sought to define their understanding of the church with reference to a series of functions, or what they called "the marks of the church." The earliest Reformers, in fact, concluded that we should look for three basic marks to identify the true church:

1. the preaching of the gospel,
2. the proper administration of the sacraments, and
3. the right exercise of church discipline.[6]

It was stated that where these three marks are clearly present, we may rest assured we have found the church of the Lord Jesus Christ.[7] In more recent times, evangelicals have likewise developed an understanding of the nature of the church based around its functions. They have listed a number of functions that should be seen as indispensable indications that a group of Christians is indeed "churching" together. While these lists can include as many as fifteen or more functions, we believe that the functions of ecclesia are captured in four primary categories—namely, worship, community, discipleship, and mission. These four functions are centered around, and serve, the defining reality of the Triune God.[8]

Figure 6.1

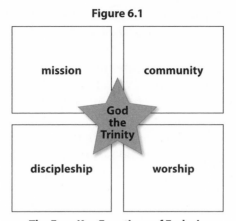

The Four Key Functions of Ecclesia

Let's look at them briefly:

1. Worship

We believe that worship is a core, indispensable, and nonnegotiable function of the church. In fact, in our campaign to encourage a missional understanding for the church, we are often misunderstood as minimizing or reducing the importance of worship in the Christian church. If we have been seen that way, it is clearly a miscommunication or misunderstanding. We wish to say in no uncertain terms that worship is an irreplaceable function in the Christian experience. We think the church should worship because our God is worthy to be worshiped. It is our response to the one holy God, who is above all. The church needs to worship. Worship isn't necessary for God; it is, however, very necessary for us, for it is only as *homo adorans*, participating in the very life of the Holy Trinity, that we become truly human. As the psychologist says in Peter Shaffer's play *Equus*, "If you don't worship, you'll shrink."

Worship therefore is not a utility but an offering, that is, a sacrifice, an economy of grace that interrupts and critiques the feverish cycles of production and consumption, which is why the collection is not fund-raising but cultural critique. If you want relevance, excitement, or profit, go to a rally, a concert, or the stock exchange. And while on this, before we boil worship down to evangelism, education, or

161

ethics, we should remember these are the possible by-products and never the motives of worship. They are blessings given as worship acts to recondition our hearts and reshape our disordered characters.

However, without diminishing the importance of the corporate praise and worship experience, we wish to also be clear that worship must be understood as being far more than a gathered worship service. As Alan has made clear in *The Forgotten Ways*, worship involves offering our world back to God. It means that bringing all aspects of life under the lordship of God *is* our central act of worship. It is our natural response to who he is and what he has done. All of life belongs to God, and true holiness and true worship means bringing all the spheres of our life under his supreme lordship.[9]

We do not deny that gathered worship meetings are a profound expression of submission to Jesus's lordship, as well as a wonderful expression of our adoration and praise for God collectively. But we must continue to remind ourselves that such worship services don't make God present. They should presuppose his presence. But God's presence is unlike any other. It is apophatic: "God does not exist," said Kierkegaard, "he is eternal." Without this God-centered apophatic point of departure, worship inevitably becomes idolatrous.

2. Community

Another irreplaceable function of the church is the painstaking and lifelong fashioning of a genuine Jesus community (or *fellowship* in a previous parlance). This is the idea expressed by the Greek New Testament term, *koinonia*. To put it crudely, if worship describes a vertical relationship between God and his people, then community is the horizontal dimension: the relationship between God's people. This would include all the communal aspects of church life: the deepening of relational bonds, the exercise of spiritual gifts, mutual encouragement and accountability, the sharing of resources, and so forth.

In Christ, we have fellowship with the family of God and with God himself. *Koinonia* is used in the New Testament to denote several aspects of our fellowship together. It can imply the sharing of the Lord's Supper (1 Cor. 10:16), the sharing of our time and energy (Heb. 13:16), and the contribution of our material possessions

(Rom. 15:26). All three usages of the word suggest a commonality of purpose, partnership, and interest.

More important, Christian community is not something about which we can arbitrarily make decisions—it is not an optional extra. One does not decide to "fellowship" with one person or another. Fellowship with other Christians is a by-product of our fellowship with God. Just as worship shows a reordering of the habits of our hearts toward God, community is the demonstration that our disordered characters have been reshaped.

This indissoluble link between fellowship with God and fellowship with his people is a key concern in John's first epistle. In 1 John 1:3 we find: "We proclaim to you what we have seen and heard, so that you also may have fellowship with us. And our fellowship is with the Father and with his Son, Jesus Christ."

3. Discipleship

Discipleship is clearly a core function of the church—heck, it's in the Great Commission itself (Matt. 28:18–20). The essential task of discipleship is to equip believers to embody the message of Jesus. Others have referred to this as *formation*: that is, the formation of individuals and the church as a whole more into the likeness of Christ. Borrowing from C. S. Lewis, we referred to this in our previous book *ReJesus* as the formation of "little Jesuses." In fact, Lewis himself said, "If the church is not doing this, then all the cathedrals, clergy, missions, sermons, even the Bible, are a waste of time."[10] Such a fashioning of little Jesuses will necessarily require the ministries of teaching, admonishment, correction, rebuke, encouragement, etc.

But the primary motivation for discipleship should come from our devotion to Jesus as Lord. In other words, submitting oneself to the process of discipleship is in itself an act of worship. It too involves offering my world back to God. Being discipled is in fact a communal activity, because no one person can be ultimately or totally responsible for the mature development of another. This was behind Paul's idea of the church as a body (see 1 Cor. 12). The gifts of the Spirit are given for the common good (1 Cor.12:7) and different people with different giftings will contribute to each person's spiritual development as a Christian. Discipleship is an activity of Christian community as well as an expression of personal worship.

Evangelicals have often placed teaching in their list of required functions, seeing the proper teaching of the Word of God as an essential part of a biblical church. We agree with the essential nature of Bible teaching, but we would rather see that reset within the broader function of the church's duty to *make disciples*. In other words, we should be less a teaching community and more of a learning community where all are on the journey of becoming mature followers of Christ. Unfortunately for many churches, their engagement with teaching can be reduced to simply listening to sermons. We would rather see the sermon as one tool among many in the development of mature disciples in Christ. Again, and not to sound defensive, we have often been misunderstood in this respect. We are not opposed to preaching at all. But we see it as a means to an end, not an end in itself. The end, if you will, is mature, godly disciples. The sermon will be part of the church's armory in equipping such disciples.

4. Mission

The fourth function the church should be committed to is mission. Others prefer to be more explicit about the aspects of mission, such as evangelism or witness, or service or social justice, but we are persuaded that the broader category of mission includes all of this. For us, *mission* is the best term for describing both the announcement of the lordship of Jesus (evangelism, witness) and its demonstration (social concern, service). Mission is not simply all the church does in service of that which is outside itself: society, culture, the environment, etc. No, mission is what the church does in service of God.[11] "Mission is more and different from recruitment to our brand of religion; it is the alerting people to the universal reign of God through Christ."[12]

Mission is the practical demonstration, whether by speech or by action, of the glorious lordship of Jesus. It is where we get to create little foretastes of the kingdom of Jesus, which has come and is still yet to fully come. If in that kingdom-to-come there will be no unbelief, then the church's mission is to create such a foretaste by commending belief to all. If in the kingdom-to-come there will be no injustice, the church's mission will be to work to eliminate injustice here and now. If in the kingdom-to-come there is no grief, no mourning, no suffering, the church's mission is to overcome such things today. Mission, then, *is* an expression of worship, for it too involves *offering our world back to God*.

The Church with Four Pillars

This might seem rudimentary ecclesiology, but it's important that we be up-front about our foundational assumptions from the outset. When we argue for a mission-shaped church, we are not saying that mission ought to take priority over worship, community, or discipleship; and we are certainly not arguing for a mission-only church, as some have presumed—we would never survive, and it would be profoundly unbiblical anyhow. We don't see how it's possible to be a church that doesn't worship, or a church without a communal life, or one that doesn't engage in discipleship and disciple making. We believe all four functions are integral to the purpose of the church as Jesus designed it to be. In fact, all these purposes, or marks, are deeply interconnected, reliant upon, and stimulated by each other.

The interconnections are obvious when you start looking for them. Jesus told his disciples, "A new command I give you: Love one another. As I have loved you, so you must love one another. By this all men will know that you are my disciples, if you love one another" (John 13:34–35). When we experience the unconditional love of Jesus, it will be expressed as love for others. Here is the indissoluble union between worship and community of which we spoke earlier. But when unbelievers observe this love, it becomes missional. Thus the Christian community witnesses to the reign of God. We defy the reader to unravel worship, community, discipleship, and mission from each other in these two verses. So too, when I feed the hungry in Jesus's name, I am worshiping God. When I shelter the homeless or visit those in prison, or when I lead a friend to Christ, it too is worship.

Need some more examples? Consider the practice of sharing the Lord's Supper. Is it an act of worship? Christians have placed its practice in the center of their worship services. It is seen, to a greater or lesser extent depending on the denomination, as a central rite, or act of worship, for the Christian community. But is it not also an expression of community? Paul is at pains to express, not only the devotional or worshipful aspect of the feast, but the communality revealed in it as well (1 Cor. 10:17). Indeed, in his teaching on the Lord's Supper, he moves back and forth between addressing it as an expression of the lordship of Jesus (worship) and an expression of the oneness of the Christian family (community).

But the practice of the communion feast could quite legitimately be seen as a missional activity. Again, Paul tells us, "For whenever you eat this bread and drink this cup, you proclaim the Lord's death until he comes" (1 Cor. 11:26). The feast has an evangelistic aspect. It is a physical, enacted proclamation of the gospel. But we hasten to add, Paul also saw it as an expression of personal and corporate discipleship. When partaking of the communion meal, we are encouraged to reflect on our journey of faith and to seek to respond to the grace of God in Jesus in a manner worthy of his sacrifice. Paul again:

> Therefore, whoever eats the bread or drinks the cup of the Lord in an unworthy manner will be guilty of sinning against the body and blood of the Lord. A man ought to examine himself before he eats of the bread and drinks of the cup. For anyone who eats and drinks without recognizing the body of the Lord eats and drinks judgment on himself. (1 Cor. 11:27–29)

This process of "examining oneself" puts personal piety and discipleship at the center of the feast. By simply taking a central biblical Christian activity as an example, we can see how all four broader functions of the church are inherently involved. We could do this for any biblically required activity. Baptism, for instance, is an act of discipleship (dying to self) and an expression of community (being baptized into the church). It is a distinctly missional activity (personal, public proclamation) and a deeply moving act of worship (offering our bodies as our true worship to God—Rom. 6, 12).

So it's not about deciding which function to put at the center—that place belongs to Jesus as Lord anyhow. Nor is it about which function is more important than the other. Besides, as we've stated, it's impossible to separate them anyway, theologically as well as in practice. For us, the question that needs to be asked is not which function should be central or should be given but rather to explore which one of them is the best catalyst for the others.

Mission as Catalysis

In chemistry a catalyst is a substance that either initiates or accelerates a chemical reaction. For any chemical process to occur, energy, known as *activation energy*, is required. Without the help of a catalyst, the amount of energy needed to spark a particular reaction is high. When the catalyst is present, the activation energy introduced makes the reaction happen more efficiently. The catalyst generally works by either changing the structure of a molecule or by bonding to reactant molecules, causing them to combine, react, and release a product or energy. For example, a catalyst is required for oxygen and hydrogen gases to combine and form water. Without the help of a catalyst, chemical reactions might never occur or take a significantly longer period of time to react.[13] When we use the term in social settings, it carries over this idea of *activating* something: we refer to something that causes an important event to happen (e.g., "the invasion acted as a catalyst to unite the country"). It is *precisely* in this sense that mission is the catalyst for the other functions—it is catalytic: it both activates the others (worship, community, discipleship) and/or makes the others work far more effectively and authentically.

We hope in this chapter to convince you of the sheer revitalizing power of mission as catalysis, but we have to admit up front that is generally not accepted in the inherited or prevailing understandings of church, or at least has not been for a very long time now. This is why the missional conversation *seems* to be such a new one. For way too long now the church has been satisfied to allow worship to act as the organizing principle of the rest. This is most evident in the way that the Sunday/weekend worship services have become the epicenter of a church's life. This is not just true as one might expect in the high/traditional churches but also in contemporary church. Most of the staff's effort, and most of the budget, goes into producing the weekend worship experiences focused on and around various demographic groups (youth, young adults, families, oldies, etc.).

This practice has deep roots in our ecclesiology. It emerged during the earliest days of European Christendom and has rarely been thoroughly critiqued—hence the dominance it plays in our idea of the church. For the more institutional church that was birthed in the fourth century and developed during the Medieval period, the Mass, which demonstrated the very presence of Christ in his church, became the center of the weekly worship gathering, and for obvious reasons: if you really believed (as the Constantinian church did) that the elements of the Eucharist were literally the body and blood of Christ, and that the ordained priest in offering the Mass was participating in a New Testament reinterpretation of temple worship, you *would* place it in the center of the community life. That's where Jesus belongs! But now it's all tied up with the priestly and churchly apparatus. When the church began to see itself as the mediating, temple-like institution interceding between God and humanity, it quickly asserted its presence in the life of the church through regular attendance at worship.

The temple always had a central role in Israel's life, and so the church, seeing itself as the new Israel, and in embedding the grace of God into the institution, developed its ecclesiology around this assumed temple-theology. But this to our mind was the deepest theological error; because by substituting itself as the Christian temple, it basically displaced Jesus's role as living, ever-present Mediator and Reconciler in the life of people. As we asserted in *ReJesus*, Jesus was/is himself the new Temple. He did everything that a temple was meant to do—providing once and for all a location where all could meet with God. When the church recasts itself as the temple, it takes on a meaning and significance that really belongs to Jesus . . . a very dangerous and idolatrous substitution indeed.

But when this incipient temple-theology wedded with the social and political power of the State, a Christian civilization emerged with the church at the spiritual epicenter—for that's where temples are, at the center. As a result, the culture was baptized, everyone became "Christian," and all were expected, often on pain of penalty or social censure, to be baptized and attend worship. When early Roman Europe became "Christianized" in this way, mission became defunct, and formal worship, maintained by priesthood, effectively trumped the other elements of the ecclesial mix. The fact that community, mission, and discipleship are not even mentioned in the "marks of the church" only proves the point—it's all about the church-based sacraments, maintained by the temple clergy, and administered largely at regular meetings.

This formalization of worship through priesthood (generally variations of sacerdotalism) is not limited to Catholicism. Even after the Reformation, Protestants still kept the worship gathering as the locus of church life, replacing the elaborate Mass with Bible teaching, communion, and baptism. By so doing, the Protestant church uncritically allowed the worship experience to retain its catalytic and determining role over all other primary functions of the church. Even teaching (a subfunction of discipleship) was located at the worship meeting and therefore subsumed under it. Community building also occurred chiefly on Sundays during or after the worship meeting and has suffered the same fate. Likewise mission, such as it has been seen throughout the past 500 years, was also centered on worship. All this lies at the basis of what we have previously called the *attractional* model of evangelism: inviting your unsaved friends to a worship service to hear the message and respond.[14]

Likewise, this makes sense of why Christians refer to the building that houses the weekly worship meeting as "the church." It leads to Christians referring to the fact that they "go to church." This phrase in itself is biblically screwy and most Christians know it, but they can't break from the default mode that tells them the worship experience organizes everything that we understand the church to be. We are so focused on the centrality of corporate worship that we cannot easily distinguish the place where we worship together from the function of worship corporately—it's a classic case of form triumphing over function.

So much is the worship seen as catalyst that in most cases planting a new church is perceived as being synonymous with launching a new worship service! The assumption is that if we start a new worship meeting, a church will emerge from that regular meeting. In other words, when we let worship do the organizing, we still end up with community and discipleship and mission, but they all emerge from, and play second fiddle to, the corporate worship dimension of church. We still, after seventeen centuries, operate largely out of a Constantinian understanding of church. Worship as organizing/ catalyzing function can be represented by the following diagram:

Figure 6.2

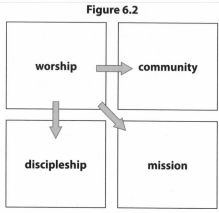

Worship as Organizing Principle

Because community and discipleship as marks or functions have rarely ever been given the catalyzing role, it's hard to point to examples as to what happens when these in fact inform and enrich the rest. Perhaps the Jesus People movement of the '60s and '70s is a good example, but even this dissolved into church-based worship with the charismatic renewal and the rise of Calvary Chapel–style teach-ins. Certainly there have been movements that have highlighted discipleship around Jesus—many reforming movements fit into this genre. When discipleship is the central function, then ethics, nonviolence, and living counterculturally become the overwhelming impulses in the life of the church. There is no question about the communal beauty in such a life—and the impact of discipleship on the quality of Christian witness. And of course disciples worship God. But we suggest that this too is not the best catalyzing function. For instance, when discipleship is not guided by the outward impulses of mission, it tends to become narrow and legalistic, and it retreats to the private pietism of "the persecuted little flock" mentality that easily infuses Anabaptist forms of ecclesia, for example. Out to the country we go, away from the contamination of worldly culture, the aim being to avoid all contact with that which defiles the purity of the pious soul. But this too inflicts a distortion in our sense of the divine purpose of the church. Is discipleship not meant to be lived as an incarnational witness at the heart of the real-time communities where people live? A retreatist spirituality is not a spirituality that can, or will, transform the world in Jesus's name.

Likewise there are movements that have emphasized the importance of community. Many of the monastic orders fit into this category. Of course worship, mission, and discipleship were a part of the equation, but they tended to serve the overall purpose of generating community. And once again, elements of Anabaptist theology lend itself to this. When the most important thing that matters is being together—when community organizes the other functions—then there is likely to be a very rich sense of relationships between brothers and sisters, but such love would always live in the shadow of the ever-present threat of its becoming the cloying, controlling community-for-its-own-sake that we critiqued in the chapter on communitas. The Christian community is meant to exist for more than itself. As William Temple once observed, the church is the only society in the world that exists for the benefit of the nonmembers.[15] We forget this to our peril.

So, we feel that we need to develop a mission-shaped view of the church, not a church-shaped view of mission. Mission as catalyzing principle might look something like this:

Figure 6.3

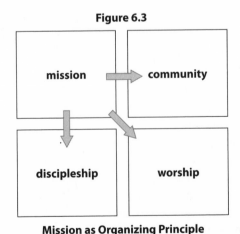

Mission as Organizing Principle

Again, we affirm that all four functions need to be present to be a healthy, fruitful, functioning church as the Bible intends it. We suggest that when mission guides and informs the others, the worship is truly understood as offering our world back to God. It becomes a world-redeeming, missional affair. When mission guides discipleship, becoming more Christlike is not just seen in narrow pietistic terms, but recognizes that in my salvation-sanctification God has laid the seeds of redemption of my world, that God's agenda works itself out through the very medium of my life. My life matters, and how I live it matters in relation to God's missional agenda, because the medium is the message. When mission guides our being with others, then we recognize that the community doesn't just exist for me, but rather that I serve Jesus in the community and that the community itself exists for the world. The church plays an irreplaceable role in God's plan of redemption. When mission guides all these, we get to show the world how to live the love of the Father, through the lordship of the Son, and in the power of the Holy Spirit.

We will try to make the case from three viewpoints:

1. theological,
2. sociological, and
3. practical.

1. Theological/Biblical

With the rediscovery of missional theology over the past century has come the awareness that the nature and character of God are best understood in terms of his mission. Indeed, the whole biblical narrative is testament to this. God is a missionary God. It is impossible to conceive of the biblical God without seeing God in terms of his mission, which is not merely the activity of God but the revelation of his very character.

David Bosch traces this missional framework for understanding God right from the creation narratives in Genesis: "In creation, God was already the God of mission, with his Word and Spirit as 'Missionaries'" (cf. Gen. 1:2–3).[16] The sending out of his Word ("and God said") to create order in the previously chaotic cosmos is a missional activity in the same way that the breathing out of his Spirit upon humankind was an expression of the *missio Dei*. Then the history of Israel is a relentless unfolding of the missionary character of God as he continued to send himself out after his people and in spite of their continued disobedience. But God's self-revelation reaches its climax in the incarnation and the resultant trinitarian formulation. Bosch continues:

> God likewise sent his incarnate Word, his Son, into the world. And he sent his Spirit at Pentecost. Mission is God giving up himself, his becoming man, his laying aside of his divine prerogatives and taking our humanity, his moving into the world, in his Son and Spirit.[17]

The mistake the church made during the Christendom period was to assume that mission was simply God's unsavory but necessary activity in a sinful world. What recent scholars like Bosch, Lesslie Newbigin, Darrell Guder, and others have helped us rediscover is that mission lies at the very center of God's nature. Bosch again:

> Mission [is] understood as being derived from the very nature of God. It [is] thus put in the context of the doctrine of the Trinity, not of ecclesiology or soteriology. The classical doctrine of the missio Dei as God the Father sending the Son, and God the Father and the Son sending the Spirit [is] expanded to include yet another "movement": Father, Son, and Holy Spirit sending the church into the world.[18]

It makes sense when put so simply. If the clearest way God chose to reveal himself to this world was by the incarnation of his Son, then it follows that the incarnation tells us a very central thing about God—he is a missionary. He is the sent and sending God. Jesus is not merely sent from the Father; he is sent as God, revealed in human terms.

Therefore it is impossible to hold to a nonmissional understanding of the God of Scripture, and it should follow that God's people should likewise be constituted by the *missio Dei*. As Leonard Sweet puts it, "The church does not define its mission. God does. It is God's mission in the world that concocts the church, not the other way around."[19]

At one level, we must understand the Trinity in missional terms. The Father sends the Son, and the Father and the Son send the Spirit. We can't only speculate on the Trinity in terms of community (three in one, working together), but in terms of sending. Therefore, if

173

God's people are a sent people, mission must be seriously considered as the organizing or catalyzing function of the church.

Basically we think mission is the catalyzing function because God is the *missio Dei*—the missionary God. The church is the net result of God's missionary activity in the world, and not only is it the recipient of God's saving mercy, but it exists to live out and extend the gospel of the kingdom in this world. In other words, God's redeeming activity in our lives is the reason why we are in the church in the first place, and mission is therefore built into the very purpose of the church.

2. Historical/Sociological

If the doctrine of the *missio Dei* is not enough to convince us of the catalyzing power of mission (and it should be), there are the unique historical and cultural challenges facing the church in the West today that force us to rethink this issue. Put simply, the church finds itself in a post-Christendom era, and it had better do some serious reflection or face increasing decline and eventual irrelevance.

In the days when people in the West believed churchgoing was a good and decent thing to do, and made assumptions about God from a broadly biblical Christian framework, inviting them back to a church service might well have been an effective form of outreach. Today, we can no longer assume unbelievers are sitting at home waiting for a better worship service to arrive in town. A church organized around worship makes the Sunday gathering the primary doorway to God, gospel, and community. And while people in a post-Christendom West might be yearning for community, having to enter via the worship service is proving to be somewhat culturally unpalatable for vast tracts of the population. Besides, the Christians aren't the only game in town anymore. If I'm overcome by existential yearning, I now have a plethora of spiritual options to try. Darrell Guder says,

> The obvious fact that what we once regarded as Christendom is now a post-Constantinian, post-Christendom, and even post-Christian mission field stands in bold contrast today with the apparent lethargy of established church traditions in addressing their situation both creatively and faithfully. Yet this helpfully highlights the need for and providential appearance of a theological revolution in missional

thinking that centers the body of Christ on God's mission rather than post-Christendom's concern for the church's institutional maintenance.[20]

Well, we hope so! In many quarters, the shrinking church constituency has been greeted by ever more energetic attempts to get people to attend on Sundays. In Britain recently, the Baptist church undertook a nationwide "Back to Church Sunday" campaign to get presumably lapsed Baptists or lapsed churchgoers to attend a worship service. In Texas, a megachurch in Houston gives away a free Wii to children who attend their kids' program and who then bring their parents to church. Another church in California gives away a Harley Davidson motorbike every year to the attendee who brings the most number of friends to church. Most churches don't have the resources for these tricks and inducements but are still bound to the imagination that church happens on a Sunday in a building. A sad expression of this attractional, service-based mission was from an Anglican church in Australia that advertised it would give a box of chocolates to anyone who would care to visit (!). It's like we are reduced to begging people to come . . . and it's not only pathetic, it borders on false witness.

If only we could discover what a church organized by mission looked like—one that saw itself as a sending church, not an in-dragging church. Sadly, it seems the situation in the West needs to get even worse for the church before its leaders come to terms with the new world in which they live. As the authors of *The Prodigal Project* say,

> The Christian church is dying in the West. This painful fact is the cause of a great deal of avoidance by the Christian community. . . . Surely God will not let his church come to death? And yet the history of the church in North Africa teaches us that we cannot assume divine intervention to maintain the status of the ecclesiastical institution. It is not only possible for Christianity in the West to falter, it is apparent that the sickness is well advanced.[21]

But as for the sheer renewing power of mission, we believe that history is on our side here. Theologians and church historians have long recognized that a movement of mission is almost always associated with, or precipitates, renewal movements in the church.[22] The Celtic missionary movement was directly linked to a deep and abiding love for God, nature, people, and learning, and birthed the Celtic monasteries that attached themselves to, and served, various villages across Ireland and later Europe. The Wesleyan revivals that started as mission and evangelism in Industrial England became the worldwide Methodist renewal of communities, discipleship, and worship. Pentecostalism, which started at the Azusa Street Mission among profoundly poor and disenfranchised people, is now a worldwide movement of over 500 million believers!

3. Practical

Third, in the light of *missio Dei* thinking and the challenges of post-Christendom, we think the contention of this book—that the adventure and risk of mission catalyzes and energizes worship, discipleship, and community—does indeed hold water. History and current experience provide many examples; the preceding chapters have made a case for this. But most readers have no further to look than your own experience. You may have undertaken some project like a short-term mission trip or have been part of a church planting team or a parachurch organization, or have participated in some form of church outreach. If so, you will know from your own experience that mission does not displace worship, or diminish the experience of Christian community or the depth of discipleship. On the contrary, if you reach into those experiences, you will find that all four functions of ecclesia were operating as they should. In the hardships and teamwork required by the mission, did you not experience rich comradeship with your brothers and sisters? Likewise, after experiencing something of what God is doing in the world, even some of God's pain for the poor and broken, did you not pray like you never had before? When people came to faith and you saw miracles, did you not worship God with all that you are? When mission is allowed to be the catalytic function, the other elements of ecclesia are not in any way diminished; they are in fact enhanced.

Not only do we believe that we cannot be a disciple without mission, and that we cannot become a true communitas without it, so too we don't think we can truly worship if we are not engaged in mission. We don't have true community in isolation from the liminal situation, and patently just worshiping God on Sundays and midweek fellowships alone does not produce disciples—because if it did actually work, then there would be no crisis of discipleship in the church. And there quite clearly is such a crisis. The Willow Creek Association, the very heart of the contemporary worship movement, pretty much admitted this in their systemwide study *Reveal*.[23] It is pertinent to note here that we are always perfectly designed to produce what we are currently producing! Mission and discipleship and communitas are patently lacking while most of our resources go into weekend services.

If worship was meant to be the catalyzing principle, as is predominantly the case throughout the West, and as many (e.g., John Piper[24]) assert, then by all accounts we should be rocking the world. Clearly, we are not. And as far as we can determine, Christianity is on the decline in every Western context. We hate to be the bearers of bad news, but apart from a very few exceptional places, non-Christian people are not exactly lining up to go to church anymore.

Let's stop kidding ourselves—there are too many instances of Christians worshiping sublimely every Sunday, but never making an impact beyond the congregation, never experiencing the powerful beauty of communitas, and never going deeper in discipleship. We think this is precisely because the catalyzing experience of missional adventure and risk are removed from the equation.

Some will no doubt argue with us on this point, insisting there must be something deficient in any worship experience if it doesn't propel people into greater godliness, greater service, greater fellowship with God and his people. Better hymns, more passionate worship, improved sermons ought to do the trick. Well, we'll have to take their word for it, but it seems academic to us. For many churches, getting worship "right" in order to catalyze mission, community, and discipleship is like trying to win the lottery. Theoretically you can win the lottery, but it rarely happens. Besides, we have to ask whether anyone in the early church was won to faith in Christ because of its great music?

We say launch a collective of believers out into the deep seas of mission and the chances are extremely high that the adventure of mission will bring to life the other core functions of the church.

Think of mission like the paddles of a defibrillator applied to the chest of a dying church. A jolt of electricity can address the lethal arrhythmias of a patient with a cardiac condition, just like a jolt of mission can catalyze the other functions of the church back to full health. As Brian McLaren says,

> For all the obvious failures of "organized religion," . . . I see the power of *organizing religion* . . . people of faith organizing for something truly beautiful and good. . . . If there is a force in the world powerful and good enough to overcome [the world], it is to be found, not in organized religion seeking institutional self-preservation, but in religion organizing for the common good.[25]

When a church embraces the call to mission, there is a ripple effect throughout every aspect of that church. Everything is shaped and directed toward the missional cause of our missional God. Instead of trying to fit God into our lives, missional Christianity asks where our lives (both individually and collectively) fit into God's mission. Instead of looking for ways to make the gospel relevant, missional churches cooperate with God's plan of transforming the world to meet the shape of the gospel. Instead of arguing about what can or cannot be included in the mission of the church, missional churches ask what kind of church God wants to shape for his mission. We may wonder about what kind of mission God has for *my church*, when we should be asking what kind of church God wants for his mission.[26]

7

The Risk of Neighborliness

An Invitation to Take the Plunge

If the Christian community has as its *eternal* goal, the goal of its pilgrimage, the disclosure of the church as city, it has as its *intermediate* goal, the goal of its mission, the discovery of the city's secret destiny through the prism of the church.

—Oliver O'Donovan

What we learn in a time of pestilence is that there are more things to admire in man than to despise.

—Albert Camus, *The Plague*

Earlier we recounted the story of how the Texan church Austin Stone reconnected with its missional mandate and in so doing reconnected with their city. We have seen this occur time and time again. To adopt a missional paradigm and embrace its associated risk almost always leads to a rediscovery of the city or town or neighborhood in which you've been placed.

On the outskirts of Phnom Penh, in what was once mosquito-infested swampland, lies a slum ominously named the Andong Re-settlement Village. It's the place where the Cambodian regime dumps all the squatters and paupers it finds on the streets of the capital after they've done their regular clean-ups of Phnom Penh. Andong is effectively a garbage dump for human refuse. Once the military have discarded them in Andong, these desperately poor families cobble together shacks made from found objects—bamboo and corrugated iron—and try to eke out an existence in the infected swamp. Following the impulse of the Spirit, one man, Pastor Abraham Hang, moved with his pregnant wife into Andong to participate in the unfolding *missio Dei*.

Michael has visited the Hangs in Andong. It's a place no Westerner would ever want to live, but it is remarkably better than when Abraham first moved in. Initially, he pulled together a working party of Christians from Phnom Penh churches to work alongside the local men to dig trenches and drain the swampland to dry out the ground and make the area habitable. Then he arranged a roster of doctors and dentists to set up mobile clinics in the slum to attend to the health and dental hygiene particularly of the children of Andong. Soon he met an American missionary, who after seeing the dreadful conditions in the slum, raised enough money from her church in Seattle to build hundreds of thatched-roof huts. Living under corrugated iron in the heat of Cambodia is almost unbearable. In their newly constructed huts they now have some semblance of comfort.

Abraham has started schools, planted churches, and with the help of Michael's church in Sydney, bought a large flat-bed truck to ferry men back and forth to Phnom Penh each day so they can find some menial labor jobs to supply a meager income. Without their own transportation, none of them could get into the city and therefore none of them could work.

In his pursuit of the *missio Dei*, Abraham has completely renovated his village. The kingdom is unfurling in Andong, and when the kingdom comes, it is evidenced by healthy children, dried-out swampland, jobs for the poor, and faith for the lost. Missional living transforms neighborhoods, not just into communities of church attenders, but into zones of justice, peace, and love.

We need to come to terms with the fact that when groups embrace the adventure and risk of mission, they will be drawn more and more deeply into the village to which God sends them. We must be all the more prepared to undertake the risk of true neighborliness.

The fact is that if Jesus's future kingdom is secure, those who trust in its coming will enact it now. With hope as our guide, we are called to fashion traces of the coming kingdom right here, and one of the primary ways to do that is by the practice of good *neighborliness*. Those with no confidence in the unfolding of Jesus's kingdom might think the present ought to be shaped by greed, injustice, exploitation, brutality, and barbarism. But the hopeful ones know that we embrace the future now by becoming better neighbors.

When asked which was the most important commandment, Jesus said, "Love God and love your neighbor." Have you ever noted that, though he is asked for the most important commandment, he gives them two? It's as if he's saying, "You cannot have one without the other. With God you always get the neighbor as well." We might live in a society that wants to separate God from neighborliness, but you can't claim to love God without loving the neighbor. In Jesus's vision of the world, they are a package deal. So, in a kingdom of neighborliness, the homeless, the widow, the orphan, the illegal immigrant, the poor, the disabled all count. They become agents of hope, opportunities for us to express our confidence in the coming kingdom, rather than threats or inconveniences.

This ought to be as true in Austin as it is in Andong. When Christian community is shaped by the risk of mission, the context for that mission takes on greater significance than in traditional, program-centered churches. Rather than developing a set of prefabricated church programs and rolling them out across the world regardless of the culture in which they are placed, missional communities take context much more seriously. Context is not only the zone in which the adventure of mission occurs, it is a distinct contributor to the shape that mission takes, because that mission is at the very least about Christian neighborliness. It provides both the social and environmental contours that form the peculiar nature of any missional community that grows there. When a missional community is prepared to embrace the risk and adventure of mission, it must be equally as prepared to embrace the risk of taking its context seriously and allowing it to, in some meaningful fashion, shape the future of the church itself.

Yet the cookie-cutter approach of the evangelical church growth movement has led to the current penchant for church franchising—the duplication of a one-size-fits-all model replete with consistency in musical style, meeting ambience, preaching, and doctrine. Everything is prefabricated; the whole venture is engineered in some head office; the approach is dictated by experts, based on their presuppositions. Nothing is indigenous, nothing feels homegrown. Nothing feels, well . . . neighborly.

Suburban Homelessness

Perhaps much of the current rootlessness of the franchise church is due to the increasing sense of homelessness experienced by its leaders, particularly those in the United States. Many American pastors, like many American professionals in general, didn't grow up where they currently work. It is nothing to meet a church leader who grew up in a small town in Texas, went to college in Michigan, attended seminary in California, and pastored or planted churches in North Carolina, Minnesota, and Virginia.

Teflon-Coated Christians

This extraordinary capacity to migrate right across a continent, apparently at home anywhere and everywhere, might at first look like just the kind of flexibility needed for missionary activity. This has been expressed to us by some leaders with the charming self-appellation: "I'm just a bloom-where-I'm-planted kind of guy." This might sound good in theory, but we think it can lead to the kind of spiritual Teflon coating that means they never actually stick anywhere. As long ago as the early 1970s, sociologist Peter Berger was pointing this out:

> Modern man has suffered from a deepening condition of "homelessness." The result of the migratory character of his experience of society and of self has been called a metaphysical loss of home.[1]

Admittedly, much of the United States was evangelized by itinerant preachers, so the itinerant lifestyle holds a certain mythic romance to many American Christians. We don't rule out that in following the *missio Dei*, many *are* called to move geographically. But we also want to sound a warning that the current obsession with migrating from one city or state to another every four or five years only reinforces to the congregations they serve that the church doesn't really "belong" in the soil in which it has been planted. If the minister could be uprooted at any time and replanted somewhere else, so could the ministry. Other countries in the West might not have the same dramatic migration pattern as the United States, but they still see their ministers moving on every four or five years, and as a result the church in the West is suffering from a sense of suburban homelessness, never at home in its local neighborhood.

Writing over twenty years ago, author and poet Wendell Berry was decrying the arrogance of property developers and industrialists who never live in the neighborhoods they create and who make decisions about the destruction of ecosystems they have never seen. Referring to these industrialist mercenaries, he says:

> The members of this prestigious class of rampaging professionals are the purest sort of careerists—upwardly mobile transients who will permit no stay or place to interrupt their personal advance. They must have no local allegiances; they must not have a local point of view. In order to be able to desecrate, endanger, or destroy a place, after all, one must be able to leave it and forget it. One must never think of one's place as one's home; one must never think of any place as anyone else's home.[2]

When churches are led by people who don't belong, who aren't really at home in the neighborhood, they generate and fund ministries that bear no relationship to the sense of place or to the potential future of that neighborhood. As Berry says of developers, the same can be said of these ministers who have no local allegiances, no indigenous points of view. In fact, it is not uncommon to find a church in conflict with its neighbors over parking issues or development applications.

A missional church sees itself as a *sent* community, and where incarnational mission is the organizing function, social context becomes an extremely important matter. In effect, a missional church identifies itself to some considerable measure as God's gift to a town or village or neighborhood. Therefore, missional churches must take seriously the rhythms of local life, the environmental and social realities of the community, and allow them to affect the kind of church that emerges there. This is another expression of communitas, the binding together of differing gifts and perspectives in the collective exercise of embedding into a culture, something way beyond the expertise or talent of any individual. Neighborliness is a corporate activity.

Staying Home

A key issue for any group willing to embrace the risk and adventure of mission is to dare to believe that they have been sent to stay home. That is, that home might be the very best place for them to serve and that the missionary call to "Go" might still apply, but it is a going *deeper*, not a going *away*. It is being sent in to every arena, domain, and context of life, not simply geographical moves. Sentness is an identity thing, not simply a geographic one.

We are anxious that our calls to adventure are not seen as implying an adrenaline-fueled, death-defying, nonstop, helter-skelter experience of life. It is truly an adventurous thing to embrace the risky call to societal engagement in our own neighborhood and to reach out, and to know and be known by the people with whom we share our roads, schools, malls, and cafés. Even those groups who have sensed God's call on their collective lives to incarnate themselves into a new neighborhood must see that that call is never completed until they have made that neighborhood truly their home. To return to Wendell Berry, he advises us quite simply,

> Make a home. Help to make a community. Be loyal to what you have made. Put the interests of your community first. Love your neighbors—not the neighbors you pick out but the ones you have.[3]

Sadly, so few churches these days are seen as doing this. The latest craze for "video-venue churches" where people gather to watch preachers beamed in via satellite from the "mother church" across town can tend to reinforce the (unintended) message that this neighborhood doesn't deserve good neighbors, only good technology. This in turn can lead to suspicion and uncertainty about new churches, with locals wondering about our motives, and assuming the church has been planted not to benefit the neighborhood but rather to benefit the growth of the denomination from which it comes.

We guess even the church members feel this sense of disconnection as well. For instance, listening to the satellite-preacher might work most of the time—well, at least until a beloved member dies or a localized catastrophe occurs, and when that Sunday's sermon makes no reference to it, we are reminded that our external preacher doesn't actually belong to our community, and we feel ripped off, spiritually and emotionally.

Finding a home and staying there is an essential skill for missional churches. It invites us to learn a dialect, discover a rhythm, and hitch our collective future to that of the village. Even those who relocate across town or around the world need to embrace the belief that they are now at home where God has placed them. They might be an "introduced species," but they are to see their function as adding value or bringing benefit to their new place.

In our homeland of Australia, cattle ranchers have introduced a type of egret as a biocontrol, for the purpose of picking ticks and flies from the skin of their cattle. You might have seen a similar bird perched on the backs of elephants and rhinoceroses in the wilds of Africa. They are doing more than hitching a ride; they eat the parasites that infect the skin of large mammals. They are an introduced species, but their contribution to the original inhabitants is beneficial. Ecologists call this mutualism. However, while the egret is a good example of this mutually beneficial introduction, its cousin (and look-alike) the oxpecker is not so. Originally thought to be an example of mutualism, oxpeckers are more likely themselves parasites. Oxpeckers do eat ticks, but often it's the ticks that have already fed on the host mammal, and there has been no proven statistically significant link between oxpecker presence and a reduction in parasite activity. In fact, it is now known that oxpeckers prefer to gouge at their host mammal's skin while searching for parasites so they too can drink the blood of their host. Our point for all this bird-talk:

missional churches must link with neighbors and be seen, like the egret, as bringing a beneficial contribution to the neighborhood.

Similarly, missional churches must consider their context like an ecosystem, an environment of interdependence and mutualism, and contribute accordingly. In her book on bioregionalism, Judith Plant says,

> Home! Remembering and reclaiming the ways of our species where people and place are delicately interwoven in a web of life—human community finding its particular place within the living and dying that marks the interdependence of life in an integrated ecosystem.[4]

The question for missional Christians is how they might be properly knitted into that interdependency of life in the integrated ecosystem of a town, village, or neighborhood. And here is where the risk comes in. Embracing our calling to integrate within the ecosystem of "home" requires what biblical scholar Walter Brueggemann refers to as an "endlessly cunning, risky process of negotiation with our world."[5]

In our travels speaking about the missional church, we are constantly asked about this aspect of missiology. How do we belong to a place without having our beliefs compromised by that community? For many church leaders, contact with place is tantamount to contamination by that place. Their presence in any particular environment is seen as an endorsement of everything that goes on in that place. We say this shouldn't be seen as such. Jesus managed to eat at the tables of sinners without endorsing all their behavior. Indeed, his presence at Zaccheaus's table evoked a dramatic display of repentance by the host. Nonetheless, we do acknowledge that missional believers must be prepared to enter into a process of ongoing negotiation with their host culture. But that seems too obvious. How do we contextualize the church in a disinterested, even hostile, culture without giving away too much at the negotiating table?

Risky Negotiation

In 1987, missiologist Paul Hiebert proposed his now well-known framework for the critical contextualization of the gospel in un-Christian contexts. His model has been embraced around the world by those involved in cross-cultural mission. It is a risky prospect, and the source of the risk is in the possibility of syncretizing the gospel, although Hiebert's model attempts to build safeguards that minimize the risk and limit that possibility. It doesn't rule them out, but it takes their possibility more seriously. The innovative aspect of Hiebert's approach is that it is based on the fundamental assumption that contextualization is a corporate venture. In other words, even the process of contextualizing the church and its message is an opportunity for communitas! The four stages are as follows:

1. Exegesis of the Culture

Hiebert proposed a thoroughgoing study of the culture into which the church is to be planted. It was his contention that the neighborhood and its culture must be examined phenomenologically by the whole church, including the newest members. It might well be that the leaders of the faith community lead the process, but such an exegesis of culture should be a communal activity. In a cross-cultural setting this means that the locals and the missionary would gather as much data about the host culture as possible, recognizing that for the missionary this will often include very new information. For missional churches in the West, it means a regular examination of our own culture, struggling against overfamiliarity and complacency. Missionaries in a new country will automatically have a wide-eyed curiosity about their new home. In the West we need to foster a similarly wide-eyed approach to exegeting our own culture.

It never ceases to amaze us how many church leaders have such little awareness of the cultural rhythms of their context. Presuming it to be just like the last town they lived in, they plow forward with little appreciation of the subtle distinctions and differences that make up the uniqueness of each and every place. When Michael first visited Houston, he asked his host, a local minister, whether they might visit the world-famous Rothko Chapel, built by John and Dominique de Menil in 1971. The de Menils founded the chapel as an intimate sanctuary for people of every belief and filled it with the mural canvasses of American abstract expressionist Mark Rothko. The chapel welcomes thousands of visitors each year, people of every faith and from all parts of the world. Indeed, the chapel has become a rallying place for all people concerned with peace, freedom, and social justice throughout the world. But Michael's host had never heard of it, even though it was just down the road from his church. Here was a marker, a secular indicator of spiritual yearning and religious harmony, but the church was oblivious to it.

As Hiebert says, we need to become curious about our own world. We need to get out of our cars and walk the streets of our neighborhood. We need to embrace our function as missionary/anthropologists and be prepared to dig into the soil in which our church has been planted. As McCartney, quoted by Marcus Curnow, says,

> The important thing for me now is to understand my place, the place in which I was born and the place in which I live. I'm slowly learning more about the natural habitat, the original inhabitants of the place and understanding that without that connection to my environment and the spiritual base of my place, I will never be able to play a useful part in the transformation of our white-centered, predominantly spiritual-less society that we call home.[6]

But as we mentioned earlier, Hiebert's genius in this respect is to insist that such an understanding be developed corporately. This is not simply the work of the clergy but of the whole faith community, who "uncritically gather and analyze the traditional beliefs and customs associated with some question at hand."[7]

Note the twofold emphasis on both congregational involvement and situation-specific questions. In Hiebert's understanding, the missionary is not the only expert; the whole Christian community becomes involved. Also, rather than a wide-ranging investigation of a particular cultural milieu (which would require the skills of an anthropologist), the locals are asked to center their inquiries on important issues raised in the day-to-day living out of faith. A congregation ought to be taken through a serious and thorough examination of certain aspects of their culture, its language, the longings of its people, its pathways of communication, etc. Hiebert emphasizes that this ought to be done uncritically. The congregation shouldn't jump to any conclusions or judgments. This step of the process involves simply listening and collating information, a difficult process for many Christians since the suspension of judgment is a rare thing in church circles.

There are real traces of this approach found in the church-growth models of American Christian leaders like Rick Warren (Saddleback Community Church) and Bill Hybels (Willow Creek Community Church). However, Hiebert is proposing something more systematic than simply asking nonchurchgoers to identify what they want in a church. He is proposing an ongoing analysis of the context in which a church exists. Therefore, a missional church will be ever involved in the gathering and analyzing of traditional beliefs and customs in their context. So rather than asking what people want in a church program and then giving it to them, the contextualizing church is always analyzing cultural shifts and trends, seeking to determine what in culture can be embraced and what must be resisted.

Hiebert encourages congregations to especially include new Christians in this process, by asking them about their beliefs and views. Again, he insists that we be prepared to suspend judgment at this point. He says,

> The purpose here is to understand the old ways, not to judge them. If at this point the missionary shows any criticism of the customary beliefs and practices, the people will not talk about them for fear of being condemned. We shall only drive the old ways underground.[8]

We are reminded here of the acerbic Australian journalist Max Harris, who once said, "Christians are a dim, ego-tripping minority which is dead set on telling everybody why they ought to become Christians, instead of finding out why they're not." Listening is justifiably part of any missional venture. In a culture where the church has been active for hundreds of years, it will serve that church well to seriously examine its own customs, language, traditions, and beliefs. Part of the church leader's role will include the questioning of long-held sacred cows, not just for the sake of iconoclasm, but with a view to intentionally contextualizing the church.

2. Exegesis of the Scripture and the Hermeneutical Bridge

In the second step, Hiebert recommends that the missionary lead the congregation in a study of the Bible related to the question at hand. When we say "second step," we don't take Hiebert to mean that the study of the Scriptures can't/shouldn't take place until a certain level of sociological research has taken place in the previous step. They are not mutually exclusive concerns. The study of the Bible and the study of culture can happen simultaneously and, as we noted earlier, as part of an ongoing process of missional engagement. That being said, Hiebert sees the missionary as having a more key role in this second aspect than in the first.

> This step is crucial, for if the people do not clearly grasp the biblical message as originally intended, they will have a distorted view of the gospel. This is where the pastor or missionary . . . has the most to offer in an understanding of biblical truth and in making it known in other cultures. While the people must be involved in the study of Scripture so that they grow in their own abilities to discern truth, the leader must have the meta-cultural grids that enable him or her to move between cultures.[9]

So the role of the leader includes the teaching of biblical truth to a local congregation. This involves the process of reminding Christians not only of what the Bible says about soteriology and Christology, but of ecclesiology. Many evangelical Christians believe a white, middle-class suburban morality is in fact ordained by Scripture and that most of the traditional practices of Protestant churches are biblical. An examination of New Testament ecclesiology would free congregations to be more open to negotiate with their host empire about their ethics, beliefs, and practices. In the same way that Peter had to reexamine his view on circumcision to allow Gentile Christians greater access to the first-century church, so does the church today have to take a good look at what the Bible says are the essentials of Christian corporate life.

3. Critical Response

Hiebert's next stage sounds easy but is in fact very demanding. After emphasizing the importance of the expertise of the missionary in the second stage, he now turns the process back to the people.

> The third step is for the people corporately to evaluate critically their own past customs in the light of their new biblical understandings,

and to make decisions regarding their response to their new-found truths.[10]

This is an important feature of his model; it is congregationally based. It is not reliant on outside experts. It validates the contribution of both new converts and older committed Christians. He says,

> [The gospel] is a message to which people must respond. . . . It is not enough that the leaders be convinced about changes that may be needed. Leaders may share their personal convictions and point out the consequences of various decisions, but they must allow the people to make the final decision in evaluating their past customs.[11]

Hiebert makes the assumption that the newer members understand their culture better than those who have been Christians for longer. If the Bible has been taught effectively and the culture examined creatively, then the Christian community must be trusted to evaluate the changes in language, customs, practices, and beliefs that need to be embraced in order to critically contextualize the gospel. It's a risk. And it involves communitas. This is where Hiebert is at his most radical. He wants the leaders to trust the congregation, believing that if the process is guided effectively, wisdom and grace will emerge. After detailed and ongoing analysis of both Scripture and culture, the church ought to be free to abandon that which is not biblical, embrace that which is, and be creatively ambivalent about that which is neither affirmed nor condemned in Scripture.

4. New Contextualized Practices

After this process, the missional church under the direction of adaptive leaders will seek to arrange the practices they have chosen, modified, and created into a new set of rituals that contextually express Christian meaning in the very context from which it emerges.

But as we warned earlier, this process is a risky one because we run into the ever-real possibility of compromising the gospel in our attempts to be contextually appropriate. We readily acknowledge this, but we also think it important to note that very often what is appropriate missionally in one context might not be in another. This is part of the church's great trauma of letting go of the one-size-fits-all

191

approach. What seems biblically justified and culturally creative in a slum in Kenya might not be so in a suburb in London. We need to allow local churches to do the work outlined above and trust them to do so responsibly. This isn't to say we can never be critical of what seems syncretistic from a distance, but we need to be prepared to sit within the context of a particular church before deeming it so.

For example, James,[12] a Baptist missionary, works in a predominantly Buddhist country in Southeast Asia. Recently a Buddhist monk from one of the nearby monasteries approached him nervously to say he had had a very vivid dream in which Jesus appeared, radiating a very loving and comforting presence. The dream ended however with Jesus telling him he had something very important to say to him. At that point he awoke! Seeking James out, the monk naively asked the missionary what Jesus might have wanted to say to him. Over several conversations, James shared the message of Jesus and eventually led the young monk in a prayer of commitment to Jesus as Lord and Savior. This young man has subsequently led a number of other Buddhist monks to faith in Jesus. So far, none of them have left their monastery. They continue to wear saffron robes, and when their fellow monks are meditating in the temple, they pray to their Lord and Master, Jesus. If the abbot insists on the performance of any activity considered unsavory to Christians, these young Christian men ask to be given the task of cleaning the monastery instead. Each week they meet with James to study the Bible and reflect on their culture in general and the culture of the monastic life in particular. They are a missional communitas, a band of brothers thrown together by faith in Jesus and working together to understand how to take both Scripture and their context seriously.

And yet, many people have been very critical of James's approach toward these new Christians. They believe he should insist that they renounce their Buddhist vows—vows of chastity, poverty, and selflessness—and leave the monastery. But James has found a home in this Southeast Asian land and understands the context. He has learned that many Asian monks are not devout Buddhists. They enter the monastery to receive a free education and to discipline their lives before embarking upon a secular career. Indeed, many leave the monastery when their term ends and attend university, looking for employment in multinational corporations. They are Buddhist by culture, not by religious conviction. These new Christian "monks," who take Jesus and faith with utmost seriousness, have far greater missional impact within the monastery than outside it.

The fear of syncretism is very real for all missional Christians, but we are heartened by Hiebert's approach in that it takes the Bible seriously and recognizes the work of the Holy Spirit in the lives of all believers. Like his contemporary Lesslie Newbigin, Paul Hiebert sees the church as a hermeneutical community, and as such the whole church must remain vigilant, actively pursuing God's will for the shape of their community. Compare this to many churches that merely comprise inactive members who attend sporadically and rely on their paid experts to do the missional work for them. Like baby birds, they attend each Sunday, their beaks wide open, awaiting a predigested meal of secondhand belief and practice. In missional churches, the baby birds have been pushed out of the nest and are learning to fly for themselves.

Missionary, Grow Home!

And yet, it should be underscored that the process of contextualization is not a short-term project. David Bosch says that one should never suggest that the church has been "enculturated," but rather that it remains in a constant state of "inculturation," a tentative and continuing process. He points out that Christendom once saw itself as the former; that is, as a singular, fully indigenized, culturally superior, completed product.[13] Today, we must come to terms with the reality that henceforth there will be a plurality of local, contextualized approaches, not any single monolithic one. Bosch called this "inter-culturation," and it is the way of the future, even as it was at our very beginning.

Urban missionary Marcus Curnow has coined an interesting turn of phrase to describe this: "The historical cry of colonized communities whose social and physical 'places' have been destroyed by a Christianity complicit with imperialism is 'Missionary go home!'"[14] Recognizing this, Curnow cleverly suggests the church should embrace a new mantra: missionary, *grow* home! In so doing, he says, we must come to terms with the "empowering and creative process of literally 'growing home.'"[15] We take him to mean that the church must see itself as God's gift to the local community and put down deep roots.

A biblical example of this connection between the church and its physical environment can be seen in Revelation 3, where John writes one of his seven letters to the Christians in Laodicea. Admittedly, it is a negative example. He begins his letter with the well-known words,

> I know your deeds, that you are neither cold nor hot. I wish you were either one or the other! So, because you are lukewarm—neither hot nor cold—I am about to spit you out of my mouth. (Rev. 3:15–16)

Many preachers have claimed that the Laodiceans were being rebuked for their lack of zeal, hence the reference to being lukewarm. However, the deeper truth is that John's message to them is an allusion to the city's unique water supply. Archaeologists have revealed that Laodicea had an aqueduct that carried water from hot mineral springs some five miles south. By the time the hot water had flowed that distance it had become tepid and, while drinkable, was hardly refreshing. By referencing the imagery of the aqueduct in his letter, John is saying something about the *usefulness* of the Laodiceans, not about their levels of enthusiasm. Whereas the hot springs at nearby Hierapolis and the pure water of Colossae are useful in their own ways, the lukewarm water at Laodicea was a symbol of the uselessness of the church there.

In a more positive sense, churches today can draw upon the natural landscape to remind themselves of their peculiar callings. Michael belongs to a missional church located on a narrow peninsula separating Sydney's North Harbor from the Pacific Ocean. Environmental concerns, particularly coastal care, are of great importance to them. They have called themselves, rather whimsically, "Small Boat, Big Sea." It says something about the physical place where God has put them, and it says something about their spiritual place on the earth, as a small community in the big sea of six billion people across the world.

If the missionary is to truly "grow home," he or she will need to reconnect with creation, protect the environment, and draw upon its symbols and seasons in the life of the church. And in a day and age where environmental degradation is such an enormous global issue and many Christians are paralyzed, not knowing what they can do to have any positive impact, the rediscovery of local context, local responsibility, and local solutions is an empowering approach.

Ethicist Gordon Preece has coined the slogan "Parish or Perish" to remind churches that they are ultimately responsible for the place to which God has called them.[16] When you visit many churches, their parking lots are crammed with the gas-guzzling SUVs of their members who have had to drive great distances to be there. If we saw our locality as being genuinely important to our missional calling, we would "church" in our own neighborhood, or relocate to the neighborhood where God wants us to serve.

We don't think this rules out translocal mission work, as adventures often involve a road of some sort, but it does give us greater perspective of what it means to participate in incarnational adventure of mission. But they probably ought to be the exception and not the rule. As we've already noted, Paul's calling was a translocal one, preaching to those Gentiles who had never heard the gospel before, as he informs the Roman church:

> So from Jerusalem all the way around to Illyricum, I have fully proclaimed the gospel of Christ. It has always been my ambition to preach the gospel where Christ was not known, so that I would not be building on someone else's foundation. Rather, as it is written: "Those who were not told about him will see, and those who have not heard will understand." (Rom. 15:19b–21)

Again, note his extraordinary claim that from Jerusalem to Illyricum—the modern-day Balkans—the gospel has been fully proclaimed. He has catalyzed a viral church-planting movement that has leapt from one continent to another. Believing his work in those regions now complete, he writes to the Romans about his intention to push even more deeply into Europe:

> But now that there is no more place for me to work in these regions, and since I have been longing for many years to see you, I plan to do so when I go to Spain. I hope to visit you while passing through and to have you assist me on my journey there, after I have enjoyed your company for a while. (15:23–24)

195

What needs to be borne in mind is that Paul is leaving indigenized churches in his wake, some in large commercial centers like Ephesus and Corinth, and others in smaller rural villages, all under the direction of indigenous leaders. While some are called to similarly translocal work today, the majority should take heed of the call to "grow home" and never despise the wonderful task of taking a communitas into the adventurous project of going deep into a neighborhood, town, or village for the purpose of contextualized mission.

Bringing It All Home

While all this talk of neighborhood and parish might seem tame and mundane, we suggest that the decision to take a group of believers deep into their own locality will lead to the inevitable risk and adventure of Christian mission. For Abraham Hang in Andong, the risks have been enormous. He has been threatened by the authorities and misunderstood by the broader Christian community. He has willingly embraced the poverty of his village. But even the venture of stepping deeply into your safe, suburban neighborhood poses a serious risk. A couple of interesting examples might bring this idea home.

In a Trailer Park in Tomball, Texas

Bob and Cathie Baldwin are a well-to-do couple who, after a stint in London where Bob worked as an executive with oil giant Enron, returned to semirural Tomball, Texas, where Cathie could indulge her love of horses on their ten-acre property. By their own admission, they were a typical Texan family. Bob was a successful corporate type, and they attended church regularly, kept a beautiful home, and enjoyed the good life in the "exurbs." The only blight on their picture-perfect life was an unsightly mobile home park a few hundred yards from their property. For the most part they managed to ignore the park and its mainly Hispanic residents, until the sewage system failed, and after complaints from the Baldwins and their other neighbors, the state authorities shut it down. Satisfied with their victory over their poor neighbors, the Baldwins assumed that would be the end of it, but the park owners eventually managed to find a way to reopen. They cut the number of mobile homes from forty to twenty and used the extra land to develop an on-site waste treatment system. The Baldwins weren't thrilled with this, but at least they had halved the size of the park.

However, some time later, the owners applied for a permit to discharge the park's treated waste into the state's water system. It was their plan to increase their capacity to fifty-five mobile homes. To the Baldwins this meant war.

At no point did Bob and Cathie stop to consider the possibility that they had any responsibility toward their poorer neighbors. They didn't ever seek, or desire, any kind of relationship with them, even though they attended church every Sunday and, no doubt, heard regularly about the gospel imperative toward neighborliness. Instead, they and their other wealthy neighbors hired an environmental lawyer and set off to fight the park owner's application. They attended hearings, wrote submissions, and briefed their legal team, but never once did they step foot inside the trailer park itself, even though it was just down the road from their home.

It wasn't until the judge hearing the case ordered them to inspect the park for themselves that the Baldwins even thought of walking through the gates and talking to the owner and the residents. What happened that day eventually changed the direction of Bob and Cathie's life. As they walked through the park, a very clear thought came to Bob, one he later believed to be from God: *If you don't like the way this park is being run, why don't you run it?* God was calling him to grow home, to see this place as his place, to embrace the missional vocation of neighborliness. But Bob was used to seeing his church as a Sunday experience and one that he drove out of town to enjoy. He wasn't ready to see church sprout from the soil of a trailer park just yet. But God had more in store for him.

In the end the judge denied the park owner's application, leaving him unable to expand his business and facing financial ruin. Shortly after, he put the mobile home park up for sale, a defeated man.

In the meantime, God brought various people across the Baldwins' path, all of whom provoked them to start reading some contemporary missiology. As Bob and Cathie continued to digest material from the missional church movement, it slowly dawned on them that God might have placed them in Tomball for a very particular reason. And Bob couldn't stop thinking about what he heard about running the park himself.

The last straw happened one Sunday when Bob looked down the pew and saw his defeated neighbor, the park owner, fellowshipping in the same church as he. This was too much for him. A deep conviction fell on him, and he realized that he was comfort-centered and self-focused, while in the Spirit he should have been mission-centered and other-focused.

> I saw myself as a comfort-worshiping idolator. I did those things, even things for God, that kept or made me comfortable. My false gods were comfort and personal peace. Like Isaiah in the presence of God, I felt ruined.[17]

Bob and Cathie went straight out and bought the trailer park. Friends of theirs, former missionaries in Latin America, moved into the manager's on-site house. Then these two families set about transforming the run-down park into a place of peace. They trimmed trees, landscaped the park, and regularly mowed the grass. They relocated the trailers that were right near a busy road further back into the park. They paved the roads and driveways, and installed streetlights and a new off-site sewage treatment system. They painted or renovated the dilapidated trailers. They built a community center in the middle of the park and ran English classes and computer skills workshops, and soon a small church started meeting there, including the Baldwins. Since then, Bob and Cathie have purchased another twenty-six acres of adjoining land. It is their intention to keep much of it untouched as a wooded play area for the local kids and to stave off the encroachment of suburbia. Their fear was that developers would level everything around them and build gated communities, leaving the trailer park isolated. They are helping to make a community. They are doing what Wendell Berry challenged us all to do: love your neighbor—not the neighbors you pick out, but the ones you have. For the Baldwins, their neighbors are 95 percent Hispanic, many undocumented, many unemployed. What they are doing with their trailer park is now spilling over to the wealthier neighbors around them who are getting onboard with helping to shape a wider community of love, grace, and truth. No one knows where this will go, but Bob Baldwin, formerly of Enron, is now a missionary in his own neighborhood, building a diverse group of locals into a marvelous expression of communitas.

Part of the problem for the traditional church today is that in many places it is not seen as being *for* the neighborhood. Like Bob Baldwin before his trailer park revelation, many churches see the social problems of their neighborhood as excuses for their judgment and condemnation, rather than as opportunities for service and partnership. If, however, churches were to take the Hiebert model of critical contextualization seriously, they would be more concerned about "reading" the culture of their neighborhood, looking for what God is saying about their neighbors.

And on the Streets of South London

Another example of this can be found in the United Kingdom, where for over fifteen years, hundreds of Christians have embraced the challenge to respond to the social needs of their neighborhoods through a missional initiative called Street Pastors. In the entertainment precincts of towns and suburbs across the United Kingdom, late-night revelers stumble out of pubs and bars in the early hours of the weekend mornings, often engaging in all manner of antisocial behavior. Given that binge-drinking, violence, and public mischief are all part of the young adult party culture across the United Kingdom, many of the local residents found that Friday and Saturday nights were like war zones right outside their homes.

But rather than condemning revelers or the licensees of the pubs, the local churches banded together to form Street Pastors, small teams of chaplains who patrol the entertainment precincts to listen to, care for, and practically help those revelers who are disoriented or distressed. Here is part of a report from England's *Telegraph* newspaper:

It is 1am on a Friday night in Sutton, a south London suburb, where 4,000 people will queue to get into—then stumble out of—bars and night clubs over the next few hours. Most are young, drunk and potentially vulnerable. Rosie has missed her last train home and wants to know where to get a night bus. Elspeth is dealing with a paralytic friend who cannot stand up. Claire is in tears because her friends used fake ID to get into a club and left her outside. There is not a policeman in sight, but help of a holier kind is at hand. I am on patrol with eight "street pastors": people so concerned about the numbers of young people out drinking that they head to high streets every Friday night to deal with the fallout. They are part of an inter-denominational Christian group of adults moving out of their middle-class, middle-aged comfort zones to make the streets feel safer while they are on patrol.[18]

Street Pastors now patrol over 100 locations across the United Kingdom and involve hundreds of volunteers of all ages, from young adults to elderly people. They are not vigilantes. They are not there to "clean up the streets." They leave law-and-order initiatives to the local police. They simply listen and care. And their presence has seen the incidence of violence and related crime drop dramatically. Politicians and community leaders have been quick to praise the Street Pastors, with London's Lord Mayor Boris Johnson calling it an "extraordinary and inspiring movement," which he sees as a key part of reducing violence on the streets.[19] David Burrowes, a member of the English Parliament, has said,

> Street Pastors is about Christians rolling up their sleeves and getting involved in practically responding to the problems of crime and safety. They are like beacons on our streets and I want to see them shining brightly in every constituency.[20]

Being on the freezing streets of an English city at 2:00 a.m., sitting in the gutter listening to a bewildered drinker, helping an intoxicated person to the taxi stand, handing a blanket to a young woman who wanted to wear a tiny strapless dress to a nightclub in the middle of winter, are all expressions of the costly, sacrificial love of Jesus. They involve risk. Street Pastors proves to residents that the church is not against the neighborhood, it is for them. It is an agent of grace and love and mercy and peace. Just as Jesus envisaged his followers would be, when he told them to let their light so shine before others, that they would see their good works and praise their God.

At the same time, each Street Pastor team is a communitas—a tight collective, united around a common goal. Whether patrolling the streets outside pubs and nightclubs or assisting drunks back home, they are bound by their common cause—to care for others and to make a safe home for all their neighbors.

Communitas, liminality, and adventure sound like exciting prospects, but sadly many Christian leaders hear these ideas in a kind of cultural limbo. But these concepts are not abstract ideas. They are possible only in the very real context of neighborhood, of locality. Going back to the missional matrix, the opportunity for communitas is possible only with the mobilization of communities of believers into societal engagement. Short-term mission trips are fine as far as that goes, but they are often manageable, bite-sized experiences to compensate us for the fact that we should see our own homes as mission fields, our own neighborhoods as liminal spaces, our own culture as the sphere of adventure to which we've all been called.

Don't Just Do Something, Sit There!

Part of the problem with the traditional approach is that the church often blunders into a neighborhood with a preconceived idea of what is wanted or needed. Often we try to simply duplicate strategies we've seen work elsewhere. If we are to do what the Baldwins or the Street Pastors or Abraham Hang have done, we need to embrace missional proximity. We need to get to know our neighborhood, intimately and without presuppositions or prejudgments. This is what Paul Hiebert was suggesting when he talks about doing exegesis on our culture.

Recently, Michael heard Stuart Murray Williams and Juliet Kilpin of Urban Expression in the United Kingdom speak on this very subject. Stuart alerted us to Jesus's use of the mustard tree as an image of the kingdom of God. He pointed out that it is not literally true, as Jesus said, that the mustard tree is the largest tree of all. Some trees like the cedar grow far taller. But the mustard tree is a sprawling, bushy shrub that sends out this massive unruly root system. It can be harder to uproot a mustard tree than a far taller cedar.

Stuart said when we look for signs of the kingdom, we often look for the big things, but maybe Jesus saw the kingdom as spreading and persistent. Stuart's advice was not to try to plant massive churches but to cultivate churches with deep roots—like a spreading weed that will not go away. A lot of traditional church-planting strategies are aimed at cultivating cedar-like trees. But if we take our neighborhood more seriously and engage more seriously in relational proximity and cultural exegesis, we could end up planting mustard bushes, deeply rooted and vastly spreading.

Juliet's advice was to reverse the old maxim, "Don't just sit there, do something." Often we launch ministries just for the sake of doing something, anything. What if we stopped doing something and just sat there in our context? Surely this would create a far richer familiarity with our neighbors, and them with us. Her suggestions included:

1. *Listen to the rhythms of your context.* Sit in local places. Hang out in local coffee shops. Talk to local people. Join community groups.
2. *Be employed in the neighborhood.* Be free of being so driven by results. Stop measuring your success by how many people attend, and start measuring it by what God is doing in your context.
3. *Engage in snowball research.* That is, meet the community gatekeepers, the movers and shakers. Listen to them. Hear of their dreams for your neighborhood. Who knows, they may be the persons of peace referred to in Luke 10.
4. *Get rid of your church building!!* Well, Juliet was being cheeky here, but she pointed out that many churches don't engage in their neighborhood because they are too locked into their building. If you got rid of it, you'd have no choice but to go and engage with the community.
5. *Say yes to every invitation you receive.* Follow Jesus's advice to his disciples in Luke 10 and accept all offers of hospitality. Say yes to every party, every meal, every committee you get invited to attend.

This last piece of advice reminds us of the Jim Carrey film *Yes Man,* in which Carrey's morose character Carl attends a self-help seminar and is told that if he simply says yes to everything, his life will be changed for the better. The word *no* must be eliminated from his vocabulary. Lonely and dissatisfied, Carl is desperate enough to accept this ridiculous challenge and ends up giving all his money to a homeless guy, learning Korean, and dating a Persian woman. But he also deepens his friendship with those he had neglected, he makes new friends, he meets the girl of his dreams, and he eventually finds success in his career.

What would happen if we as Christians took the risk of saying yes to everything? What groups would we join? At whose table would we find ourselves eating? What adventures would we end up having? Whenever we've posed this question to groups or classes, we find it is met with some resistance by a few Christian leaders. What, they ask, would we say if invited to visit a strip club or to watch pornography? But we wonder why church leaders always assume these worst-case scenarios. Of course, we should resist invitations to illicit behavior, but our educated guess is that you'll be invited to a great many more innocent activities before something like that comes up.

Michael recently met a Baptist minister in Oregon who had been regularly invited by his neighbor to join him and several other men of his street for a margarita in the shed in his backyard. Apparently his neighbor concocted famous homemade margaritas, and all the neighborhood men regularly gathered to drink them and chill out in his "man cave." After politely rejecting the offer several times, the Baptist minister finally agreed, and a whole new missional world opened up to him.

In Bangalore, India, an English missionary working and living in a slum community was invited to join a committee to lobby the city to provide the slum with a post box. Initially, he considered this a trivial matter and unworthy of his higher calling to preach the gospel, but he reluctantly agreed, thinking it a simple clerical assignment. It turned out that the slum wanted a post box because that would provide them with a postal code (or zip code), which would make them a bona fide neighborhood, which would mean the authorities couldn't evict them anytime they liked. By saying yes to this challenge, he was drawn into an eighteen-month-long struggle with the city hall. He was beaten up. He was scorned and mocked. But he found a powerful solidarity with his neighborhood, and when he finally helped them secure their post box, he knew he had entered into this community more deeply and more missionally than if he'd simply gone about the slum preaching.

In the East Bay Area of northern California, two young men heard us speaking about missional living and decided to go to their nearest Burger King and distribute coupons for free burgers to the homeless and the indolent young men who hung around the parking lot. One hungry man was so grateful for the free burger, he invited the two young Christians to join him in a bowling competition at a nearby pub. Nervous about accepting this invitation because they didn't drink, and mindful of the sermons they'd heard in their church about not entering such premises, they agreed tentatively. They now have more nonchurch friends than ever and have managed to share their faith and offer acts of kindness on scores of occasions.

With all our talk of risk taking and adventure we might have inadvertently given the impression you needed to jump off a cliff or move to the darkest part of the Amazon to be missional, but we firmly believe that it takes courage to simply say yes to the requests and invitations of our neighbors. We firmly believe the mission field is in Phnom Penh, Cambodia, and Bangalore, India, but it's also in your next-door neighbor's shed or the local Burger King. We've seen people finding their mission field in a bar in Birmingham, England; in a bead shop in Glasgow, Scotland; in an art gallery in Sydney, Australia; and in a cul-de-sac in Edmonton, Canada.

We firmly believe that when a community of believers embraces the challenge to move out from within themselves, to serve others, to listen to others, to help build a home where God sends them, and to announce that the kingdom is at hand in word and deed, the true essence of what it is to be the people of God can be experienced in all the richness and beauty and messiness and joy as it was originally intended.

The Beginning of the End

Conclusion

The trick of finding what you didn't lose, is arriving at the place you never left.

—e. e. cummings

A soldier fears he is a coward. Is he? Only if he acts like one. His action will proceed not from a pre-defined nature but from the choices he makes when the bullets start to fly.

—J. W. Sire

And so we have come to the end of our book. When a book is written, the author, or authors in this case, do actually have some sort of idea of what they want to say, and they do follow a plan. But a book, fiction or nonfiction, does tend to take on a life of its own. Call this the work of the Spirit or simply whim, this book evolved from being a book designed to elaborate on the idea of communitas and missional church to becoming a book that is more akin to a theology of adventure and an apologetic for risk.

Without claiming too much in this, we do believe that this shift in emphasis has been a work of the Spirit through our all-too-human lives. We think this is the case because adventure—our capacity to engage fully in the open-ended journey that is the church of Jesus

Christ—is the atmosphere out of which many ideas of missionality are formed. As a category of existence, it is actually *prior* to any discussion about missional church models and practices, because God is a God of adventure, and a life well lived, a life of discipleship, must be one that can take risks as we courageously follow our Lord. This is what we call the faith of leap.

Conversely, our failure to engage the adventure of the spirit/Spirit that is the gospel, and our subsequent risk aversion, have deeply damaged the nature of our witness as well as our experience of authentic *ecclesia*—the church that Jesus built.

Our adventure, at least this earthly stage of it, does not stop until God determines in the fullness of time to bring everything to completion in the consummation of all things. But if, as we argue here, this adventure is a category that equally describes God, then we doubt it will stop once Jesus returns to redeem his people. Adventure will be part of our continued experience of life in God. Heaven will not be a place where all life as movement and growth will cease and all that we will do is sit on clouds and play harps in some sort of perpetual Sunday worship experience. Well, at least we really hope not, because that would be a serious anticlimax!

If God is the *missio Dei*, the missionary God, and if redemption is an intrinsic aspect of his nature and being, then whatever heavenly existence we will experience then must still involve something of this aspect of God. Life, and particularly life in God, will always involve dynamic movement, growth, development, change, participation . . . *adventure*. In other words, to co-opt the language of philosophy, adventure is not just an existential phenomenon; it has ontological status. If heaven is an adventure, we had better get used to it and get into it, because there is going to be a lot of it to come.

And the church, the redeemed people who follow Jesus the great Adventurer, archetypal Hero, apocalyptic Rider, and courageous Savior, ought to be a place where there is great adventure and the risk of faith and mission—for to love God is to become like him. If this is not the case, we have good cause to question whether we have truly encountered Jesus and are worshiping the right God.

Christianity is an adventure of the spirit or it is not Christianity. We must repent of our obsession with safety and security and do the task that only we as Jesus's people can do. And so we finish with something of a creedal affirmation that for us sums up something of the call to adventurous mission and discipleship.

> I would rather be ashes than dust!
> I would rather that my spark should burn out in a brilliant blaze than it be stifled by dry rot.
> I would rather be a superb meteor, every atom of me in magnificent glow, than a sleepy and permanent planet.
> The proper function of man is to live, not exist.
> I shall not waste my days in trying to prolong them.
> I shall use my time.
>
> —Jack London

Notes

The End of the Beginning: Introduction

1. See Matthew 6:9–10; 16:19; Mark 11:24; John 14:13; 16:23, 26.

2. J. R. R. Tolkien, *The Two Towers: The Stairs of Cirith Ungol*, The Lord of the Rings (New York: Random House, 1973), 362.

3. Ralph C. Wood, *The Gospel According to Tolkien: Visions of the Kingdom in Middle-earth* (Louisville: Westminster John Knox, 2003), 45–47.

4. Quoted in ibid., 45.

5. Ibid., 46.

6. Ecclesiology, in turn, must always recalibrate back to Christology.

7. Stuart Murray, *Church after Christendom* (Carlisle, UK: Paternoster, 2005), 19.

8. From Stuart Murray's article, "Post-Christendom, Post-Constantinian, Post-Christian . . . does the label matter?" www.postchristendom.com/files/Does%20the%20label%20matter .pdf.

9. David J. Bosch, *Transforming Mission: Paradigm Shifts in Theology of Mission* (Maryknoll, NY: Orbis, 1991), 2–3, italics added.

10. Attributed to Hans Küng, quoted in Alan Hirsch, *The Forgotten Ways: Reactivating the Missional Church* (Grand Rapids: Brazos, 2007), 15.

11. See our book *ReJesus: A Wild Messiah for a Missional Church* (Peabody, MA: Hendrickson, 2009) for a thorough exploration of the significance of Jesus for the ongoing mission and vitality of the church.

12. Wood, *Gospel According to Tolkien*, 46.

13. J. R. R. Tolkien, *The Fellowship of the Ring*, quoted in Wood, *Gospel According to Tolkien*, 46.

Chapter 1 The Spirit's Edge

1. D. H. Lawrence, "Escape."

2. The religious dimension heightens the sense of existence to an immeasurable degree. For instance, "the sliding of our existence over a scale on which every point is simultaneously determined by the effect of our strength and our abandonment to impenetrable things and powers—this problematic nature of our position in the world, which in its religious version results in the insoluble question of human freedom and divine predetermination,

lets all of us become adventurers." Georg Simmel, *The Adventure* #27. http://condor.depaul
.edu/~dweinste/theory/adventure.html. Originally published as "Das Abenteuer," *Phioso-
phische Kultur. Gesammelte Essays*, trans. David Kettler, 2nd ed. (Leipzig: Alfred Kroner,
1919).

3. MyHeroProject, *My Hero: Extraordinary People on the Heroes Who Inspire Them*
(New York: The Free Press, 2005), 79.

4. C. S. Lewis, "Learning in Wartime," *C. S. Lewis: Essay Collection and Other Short
Pieces* (London: HarperCollins, 2000), 579–80.

5. Jacques Ellul, *The Subversion of Christianity* (Grand Rapids: Eerdmans, 1986), 168.

6. C. S. Lewis, *The Screwtape Letters* (London: HarperOne, 2001), 137–38, italics added.

7. Scott Bader-Saye, *Following Jesus in a Culture of Fear* (Grand Rapids: Brazos, 2007), 67.

8. See for instance John Sanders, *The God Who Risks: A Theology of Providence* (Downers Grove: InterVarsity, 1998); Gregory Boyd, *God of the Possible: A Biblical Introduction
to the Open View of God* (Grand Rapids: Baker, 2000); and Clark Pinnock, ed., et al., *The
Openness of God: A Biblical Challenge to the Traditional Understanding of God* (Downers
Grove: InterVarsity, 1994). Opponents of open theism include John Piper et al., *Beyond the
Bounds: Open Theism and the Undermining of Biblical Christianity* (Wheaton, IL: Cross-
way, 2003); and Millard J. Erickson, *What Does God Know and When Does He Know It?
The Current Controversy over Divine Foreknowledge* (Grand Rapids: Zondervan, 2006).

9. Simmel, *The Adventure*.

10. David Bosch, *Believing in the Future* (Valley Forge, PA: Trinity Press, 1995), 33.

11. John P. Kotter, *Leading Change* (Harvard: Harvard Business Press, 1996).

12. John P. Kotter, *A Sense of Urgency* (Harvard: Harvard Business Press, 2008).

13. Ibid., 16.

14. Ibid., ix.

15. Ibid., 170.

16. Ibid., 58–59.

17. Ibid., 47. Furthermore he notes in chapter 3 that tactics that aim at the heart have
five key characteristics:

1. They are thoughtfully created human experiences (not just documents and abstract
ideas).

2. They work on all the senses, not just the ears. They can be compelling, surprising,
or dramatic in ways that influence our emotions.

3. They elicit the right kinds of emotions and make people feel that they can accomplish what is needed, that the crisis can be an opportunity.

4. The experience does not need an explanation. It is not covert or manipulative but
it avoids saying in words what is difficult to say or hear.

5. It leads us to raise our sights and to emotionally embrace new goals (47–49).

18. Ibid., 126.

19. Ibid., 132, 135.

20. Ibid., 185.

21. Thomas A. Kolditz, *In Extremis Leadership: Leading As If Your Life Depended on
It* (San Francisco: Jossey-Bass, 2007), 20–21.

22. Ibid., 41.

23. Ibid., 71.

24. Ibid., 50–51, 87.

25. Louis Jacobs, *Jewish Preaching* (Portland, OR: Vallentine Mitchell, 2004), 80.

26. Saying ascribed to Andre Malraux. Source unknown.

27. Donald Kuratko, *Entrepreneurship: Theory, Process, Practice* (Mason, OH: Cengage Learning, 2009), 6.

28. Paul Waddel, *Friendship and the Moral Life* (Notre Dame: University of Notre Dame Press, 1989), 164.

29. Bader-Saye, *Following Jesus*, 73.

Chapter 2 Jesus Is My Disequilibrium

1. Bader-Saye, *Following Jesus*, 69.

2. Alison Morgan, *The Wild Gospel* (Oxford: Monarch Books, 2004), 189.

3. Ibid., 189.

4. Bader-Saye, *Following Jesus,* 70.

5. Ibid., 69. He goes on to note that "Anglican theologian John Milbank argues that 'virtue cannot properly operate except when collectively possessed.' This is never truer than when talking about courage. Courage requires community, both for the learning of courage and the living of it. And this community is not just of the present, but of all those who have gone before us. In the reading of Scripture and the remembrance of the saints, we recall all those who have embodied courage in the past. We remember them and pray for the strength to imitate them" (69).

6. This chapter is a summary of what we have previously written and is drawn largely from *Exiles* (Peabody: Hendrickson, 2006) 108–25, and *The Forgotten Ways* (Grand Rapids: Brazos, 2007), chap. 8.

7. See Victor Turner, *The Ritual Process: Structure and Anti-Structure* (Ithica, NY: Cornell University Press, 1969), and "Passages, Margins, and Poverty: Religious Symbols of Communitas," part I, *Worship* 46, nos. 7 and 8.

8. See Turner, *The Ritual Process*, 129. He calls communitas anti-structure because the participant finds himself outside of the normal structured existence of the community as he knew it.

9. Cf. Richard Rohr, *Adam's Return: The Five Promises of Male Initiation* (New York: Crossroad Publishing Co., 2004).

10. Victor Turner, *From Ritual to Theatre: The Human Seriousness of Play* (New York: PAJ Publications, 1982), 45.

11. Richard L. Celsi, "Transcendent Benefits of High-Risk Sports," *Advances in Consumer Research*, eds. John F. Sherry Jr. and Brian Sternthal (Provo, UT: Association for Consumer Research, 1992), 19:636–41, http://www.acrwebsite.org/volumes/display.asp?id=7366.

12. Ibid.

13. Ibid.

14. Ibid.

15. Paul S. Minear, *Images of the Church in the New Testament* (Philadelphia: Westminster, 1960), 62.

16. Scott Nash, *The Church as a Pilgrim People: Hebrews-Revelation* (Macon, GA: Smyth & Helwys, 2001).

17. Nash, *Church as a Pilgrim People*, http://www.helwys.com/bookexcerpts/pilgrim_people_excerpt.html.

18. Ibid.

19. Ibid.

20. Quoted at "A Place of Transition," http://www.creativeresistance.ca/communitas-toc.

21. Quoted in Robert Bly, *Iron John* (London: Element Books, 1991), 155.

22. http://www.thewinkingcircle.com/story.htm.

23. Richard Rohr, "Boys to Men: Rediscovering Rites of Passage for Our Time [Richard Rohr]," Family, John Mark Ministries, Jan. 5, 2003, http://jmm.aaa.net.au/articles/5358.htm.

24. Heinrich Zimmer, quoted in Rohr, "Boys to Men." We are indebted to Richard Rohr, who has helped the church understand the power of ritual particularly in forming boys to men. See his "Boys to Men" article.

25. Blake Carter Hope Evangelical Free Church, Communitas, vol.10, no. 3: 1–2; http://www.hope-church.ws/uploads/documents/newsletter/4_Communitas2005_10.pdf.

Chapter 3 A Walk on the Wilder Side

1. Alex Ayres, The Wisdom of Martin Luther King, Jr. (New York: Meridian, 1993).

2. Blaise Pascal, Pensees, #233. See, for example, Stanford Encyclopaedia of Philosophy, http://plato.stanford.edu/entries/pascal-wager/.

3. C. S. Lewis, The Four Loves (New York: Harcourt Brace, 1960), 21.

4. Bosch, Transforming Mission, 519.

5. Elton Trueblood, The Common Ventures of Life (New York: Harper, 1949). Full e-text, http://tinyurl.com/ydvcn2w.

6. Bosch, Transforming Mission, 9.

7. Bader-Saye, Following Jesus.

8. Ibid., 31.

9. Ted Peters, Sin: Radical Evil in Soul and Society (Grand Rapids: Eerdmans, 1994), chap. 2.

10. Ibid., 28.

11. Ibid., 26.

12. Ibid., 13–14.

13. Bader-Saye, Following Jesus, 13–14.

14. Ibid., 31, 59.

15. About the fear of God, Bader-Saye says, "If we can experience that power close-up and not be gripped in our guts by the disparity between God and ourselves, then we are in a profound state of spiritual slumber, if not acute mental illness." Ibid., 43–44.

16. Quoted in Michael Yaconelli, Messy Spirituality: God's Annoying Love for Imperfect People (Grand Rapids: Zondervan, 2002), 87.

17. Hans Urs Von Balthasar, The Christian and Anxiety, trans. D. D. Martin and M. J. Miller (San Francisco: Ignatius Press, 2000), 88.

18. Bader-Saye, Following Jesus, 60

19. Mary Cholmondeley, quoted in J. LeBron McBride, Pastoral Care from the Pulpit: Meditations of Hope and Encouragement (Birmingham: Haworth Pastoral Press, 2007), 77.

20. Alan Hirsch and Debra Hirsch, Untamed: Reactivating a Missional Form of Discipleship (Grand Rapids: Baker, 2010). In many ways Untamed as a whole is framed around what we called Shema spirituality. We encourage the reader to explore the centrality of this for worship, mission, and discipleship there.

21. St. Augustine, Confessions, trans. M. Boulding (New York: Vintage, 1997), 62.

22. Lewis, The Four Loves, 21.

23. Quoted in Dallas Willard, The Spirit of the Disciplines: Understanding How God Changes Lives (New York: HarperCollins, 1988), 7.

24. Morris L. West, The Shoes of the Fisherman (New York: Morrow, 1963), 254.

25. Lewis, The Four Loves, 122.

26. John Eldredge, Wild at Heart: Discovering the Secret of a Man's Soul (Nashville: Thomas Nelson, 2001).

27. See Richard Rohr with Joseph Martos, *From Wild Man to Wide Man: Reflections on Male Spirituality* (Cincinnati: St. Anthony, 2005); and Robert Bly, *Iron John: A Book about Men* (Cambridge: De Capo, 2004).

28. Clarissa Pinkola Estes, *Women Who Run with the Wolves* (London: Random House, 1992).

29. Ibid., 4.

30. Douglas Coupland, *Generation X* (New York: St. Martins, 1991), 147.

31. Stephen Lyng, ed., *Edgework: The Sociology of Risk-Taking* (New York: Routledge, 2005), 23.

32. Ibid.

33. As quoted in Joan Aho Ryan, *Lessons from Mom: A Tribute to Loving Wisdom* (Deerfield Beach: Health Communications, 1996), 69.

34. See http://www.kurthahn.org/writings/writings.html. The summary is drawn largely from the article on Hahn's philosophy in http://en.wikipedia.org/wiki/Kurt_Hahn.

35. Niccolò Machiavelli, *The Prince*, trans. Luigi Ricci (Fort Worth: Lulu, 2008), 22.

36. Sally G. McMillen, *Seneca Falls and the Origins of the Woman's Rights Movement* (Oxford: Oxford University Press, 2008), 70.

37. Abraham Heschel, *Man Is Not Alone: A Philosophy of Religion* (New York: Noonday Press, 1990), 259.

38. "Albert Einstein," *Life* 38, no. 18 (May 2, 1955): 64.

39. Quoted in Milton Meltzer, *Albert Einstein: A Biography* (New York: Holiday House, 2008), 5.

40. John C. Maxwell, *Failing Forward: Turning Mistakes into Stepping Stones for Success* (Nashville: Thomas Nelson, 2007).

41. Summary taken from ibid., 27–30.

42. Story told in Hirsch, *The Forgotten Ways*, chap. 1.

43. http://www.fastcompany.com/magazine/37/tyler.html?page=0%2C2.

44. Antony Alpers, *Katherine Mansfield: A Biography* (New York: W. W. Norton, 1983), 341.

Chapter 4 The Hero's Journey

1. See Hirsch, *The Forgotten Ways*, chap. 6. Also see Alan's forthcoming fall 2011 book tentatively titled *The Permanent Revolution: Apostolic Imagination and Practice for the 21st Century Church* (San Francisco: Jossey Bass, 2011) for a comprehensive description of the apostolic ministry.

2. Joseph Campbell, *The Hero with a Thousand Faces* (Novato, CA: New World Library, 2008), 23.

3. Summary from Christopher Vogler, *The Writer's Journey: Mythic Structure for Writers* (Studio City, CA: Michael Wiese Prod., 2007).

4. Lynne White, quoted in P. S. Minear, *Eyes of Faith: A Study in the Biblical Point of View* (Philadelphia: Westminster, 1946), 106–7.

5. C. S. Lewis, "Tolkien's Lord of the Rings," *Essay Collection & Other Short Pieces* (London: HarperCollins: 2000), 525–26.

6. Ibid., 524.

7. Ibid..

8. C. S. Lewis, *The Weight of Glory* (London: HarperCollins, 1980), 43.

9. L. W. Dorsett, ed., *The Essential C. S. Lewis* (New York: Touchstone, 1988), 363.

10. Ibid.

11. Quoted in Wayne Martindale and Jerry Root, eds., *The Quotable Lewis* (Wheaton: Tyndale, 1989), 444–45.

12. Colin Greene and Martin Robinson, *Metavista: Bible, Church and Misison in an Age of Imagination* (Carlisle, UK: Paternoster, 2008), 196.

13. Adapted from Collin Greene and Martin Robinson, Metavista: Bible, Church and Mission in an Age of Imagination, Faith in an Emerging Culture series (Carlisle, UK: Paternoster, 2008), 196. For information on APEST, visit www.theforgottenways.org/apest.

14. Ibid., 201.

15. Ibid.

16. Bosch, *Transforming Mission*, 67.

17. Greene and Robinson, *Metavista*, 202.

18. Ibid., 203.

Chapter 5 Getting Over Risk Aversion

1. Richard Pascale, Mark Milleman, and Linda Gioja, *Surfing the Edge of Chaos: The Laws of Nature and the New Laws of Business* (New York: Three Rivers, 2000), 61.

2. Ibid., 6.

3. Ronald A. Heifetz and Donald L. Laurie, "The Work of Leadership," HBR Classic, *Harvard Business Review*, Dec. 2002.

4. Peter Bernstein, *Against the Gods: The Remarkable Story of Risk* (New York: John Wiley & Sons, 1998), 34.

5. Ibid., 53.

6. Ibid., 106.

7. Reuben Feffer, in *Along Came Polly*, Universal Studios, 2004.

8. See also Matthew 10:39; 16:26; Mark 8:35; Luke 9:24; John 12:25.

9. Gregory A. Boyd, *The Myth of a Christian Religion: Losing YourReligion for the Beauty of a Revolution* (Grand Rapids: Zondervan, 2009), 168.

10. Ibid., 168.

11. Ibid.

12. Ulrich Beck, *Risk Society: Towards a New Modernity* (London: Sage Publications, 2000), 183.

13. Ibid., 21.

14. Erwin McManus, *The Barbarian Way: Unleash the Untamed Faith Within* (Nashville: Thomas Nelson, 2005), 117.

15. Ibid., 122.

16. Pascale et al., *Surfing the Edge*, 20.

17. Ibid.

18. Michael Frost and Alan Hirsch, *The Shaping of Things to Come: Innovation and Mission for the 21st-Century Church* (Grand Rapids: Baker, 2004), 194. See also Harvey Cox, quoted in *The Annals of the American Academy of Political and Social Science*, ed. Wade Clark Roof, vol. 480, Religion in America Today (Thousand Oaks, CA: Sage, 1985), 50.

19. Adapted from Pascale et al., *Surfing the Edge*, 40.

20. Lyng, *Edgework*, 5.

21. Ibid., 9–10.

22. Ibid., 10.

23. Ibid., 6.

Chapter 6 Missional Catalysis

1. For the basic story, go to http://www.austinstone.org/who/church_history/.

2. Roland Allen, *The Spontaneous Expansion of the Church* (Cambridge, UK: Lutterworth, 2006), chap. 8.

3. Ibid.

4. Ibid.

5. Frost and Hirsch, *The Shaping of Things to Come*, 193.

6. The marks of the church are treated in the Confession of the English Congregation at Geneva (1556); the French Confession of Faith (1559), articles 26–28; the Scottish Confession of Faith (1560), chapters 16 and 18; the Belgic Confession of Faith (1561), articles 27–29; Second Helvetic Confession (1566), chapter 17.

7. In the following discussion, our comments are narrowly focused upon the identity of the true church in an institutional sense. Because the believer's connection to the institutional church comes within the context of the local congregation, that is the focal point of our inquiry. In an enlarged discussion of related themes, we could explore the differences between the visible church and the invisible church. The Scriptures clearly make a distinction between the universal church of all ages, the elect, "the heavenly Jerusalem the general assembly and church of the firstborn, which are written in heaven" (Heb. 12:22–23) and the local congregations which are composed of those in outward communion with the assemblies of Christ. Thus, the historic Protestant creeds distinguish between the visible church and the invisible church (cf. Westminster Confession [1646], chapter 25; the Scottish Confession of Faith [1560], chapters 16 and 18). Obviously our discussion pertains mainly to the visible church, regarding its proper identification: that is, how it may be discerned among local congregations.

8. This is not the place to explore our belief that the central confession of the church remains "Jesus is Lord!" and is therefore primarily Christological in nature. We worship the Father, through the Son, and in the power of the Spirit. For thorough examination of this, see our book *reJesus*.

9. See Hirsch, *The Forgotten Ways*, 90–92.

10. W. Vaus, *Mere Theology: A Guide to the Thought of C. S. Lewis* (Downer's Grove: InterVarsity, 2004), 167.

11. Bosch defines mission this way: "Mission takes place where the church, in its total involvement with the world, bears its testimony in the form of a servant, with reference to unbelief, exploitation, discrimination and violence, but also with reference to salvation, healing, liberation, reconciliation and righteousness. Mission is not competition with other religions, not a conversion activity, not expanding the faith, not building up the kingdom of God; neither is it social, economic, or political activity. And yet, there is merit in all these projects. So, the church's concern *is* conversion, church growth, the reign of God, economy, society and politics—but in a different manner! The [mission of God] purifies the church. It sets it under the cross—the only place where it is ever safe. The cross is the place of humiliation and judgment, but it is also the place of refreshment and rebirth. . . . Looked at from this perspective mission is, quite simply, the participation of Christians in the liberating mission of Jesus, wagering on a future that verifiable experience seems to belie. It is the good news of God's love, incarnated in the witness of a community, for the sake of the world." Bosch, *Transforming Mission*, 519.

12. Ibid.

13. See, for example, http://www.wisegeek.com/what-is-a-catalyst.htm.

14. Discussed in *The Shaping of Things to Come* and *The Forgotten Ways*.

15. Quoted in Philip Yancey, *Church: Why Bother?* (Grand Rapids: Zondervan, 1998), 31.

16. David J. Bosch, *Witness to the World: The Christian Mission in Theological Perspective* (Eugene, OR: Wipf and Stock, 2006), 239.

17. Ibid.

18. Bosch, *Transforming Mission*, 390.

19. Leonard Sweet, *Carpe Mañana: Is Your Church Ready to Seize Tomorrow?* (Grand Rapids: Zondervan, 2001), 27.

20. Darrell Guder, ed., *Missional Church: A Vision for the Sending of the Church in North America* (Grand Rapids: Eerdmans, 1998), 7.

21. C. Kirkpatric, M. Riddell, and M. Pierson, *The Prodigal Project: Journey into the Emerging Church* (London: SPCK, 2000), 3.

22. See Howard A. Snyder, *Signs of the Spirit: How God Reshapes the Church* (Grand Rapids: Academie, 1989) and *Models of the Kingdom* (Eugene: Wipf & Stock, 2001). For general reference of mission as the catalyzing principle of renewal and advancement in the church, see, for instance, Kenneth Scott Latourette, *A History of the Expansion of Christianity*, 7 vols. (New York: Harper & Brothers, 1945).

23. For a list of *Reveal* resources, see http://www.revealnow.com.

24. John Piper, *Let the Nations Be Glad: The Supremacy of God in Missions* (Grand Rapids: Baker, 1993).

25. Brian McLaren, *Everything Must Change* (Nashville: Thomas Nelson, 2007), 265.

26. A variation of the question posed by Christopher Wright, *The Mission of God: Unlocking the Bible's Grand Narrative* (Downers Grove: InterVarsity, 2006), 534. The preceding paragraph is based on a series of bullet points that Wright includes in the conclusion to his book, 533–34.

Chapter 7 The Risk of Neighborliness

1. Peter Berger, *The Homeless Mind: Modernization and Consciousness* (Penguin, 1974), 77.

2. Wendell Berry, "Higher Education and Home Defense," *Home Economics* (San Francisco: North Point Press, 1987), 7.

3. Wendell Berry, "The Futility of Global Thinking," *Harpers*, September, 16, 1989, 22.

4. Judith Plant, *Healing the Wounds* (Vancouver: New Society Publishers, 1989), iii.

5. Walter Brueggemann, *Cadences of Home* (Louisville: Westminster John Knox Press, 1997), 11.

6. Quoted in Marcus Curnow, "Missionary Grow Home!" *Zadok Perspectives*, Zadok Papers, S167, Autumn 2009, 11.

7. Paul Hiebert, "Critical Contextualization," *International Bulletin of Missionary Research* 11 (July 1987): 109.

8. Ibid., 109.

9. Ibid., 110.

10. Ibid.

11. Ibid.

12. Pseudonym used to protect his privacy.

13. Bosch, *Transforming Mission*, 456.

14. Curnow, "Missionary Grow Home!" 16.

15. Ibid.

16. Gordon Preece, "Parish or Perish: the Church as a Community in the Community," *Southern Cross*, July 1987, 8–10.

17. Faithwalking manual, 97. Cited at http://www.faithwalkingonline.com/.

18. Rowena Mason, "Street pastors making a difference after-hours," *The Telegraph* online version, Friday, 1 June, 2008, http://www.telegraph.co.uk/news/uknews/2059652/Street-pastors-help-young-revellers-on-their-way.html.

19. Ibid.

20. Street pastors website, http://www.streetpastors.co.uk/Home/tabid/255/Default.aspx.

Michael Frost is an internationally recognized Australian missiologist and one of the leading voices in the missional church movement. His books are required reading in colleges and seminaries around the world, and he is much sought after as an international conference speaker.

Michael is the vice principal of Morling College and the founding director of the Tinsley Institute, a mission study center located at Morling College in Sydney, Australia. He is the author or editor of ten theological books, including *Jesus the Fool*, *Seeing God in the Ordinary*, and *Exiles*. These books explore a missional framework for the church in a postmodern era. Their popularity has seen him regularly speaking at conferences in the US, the UK, and across Europe, and as far afield as Nairobi, Rio de Janeiro, and Moscow.

He is the founder of the missional Christian community *smallboatbigsea*, based in Manly in Sydney's north, and the weekly religion columnist for *The Manly Daily*. He helped establish Action Against Poverty, a localized microfinancing agency, linking the cities of Manly and Manado, an impoverished Indonesian community. Michael was also instrumental in launching Street Pastors in Sydney, an incarnational ministry aimed at reducing the effects of alcohol-related violence in entertainment precincts.

Alan Hirsch is the founding director of *Forge Mission Training Network*. He is the cofounder of shapevine.com, and currently he leads an innovative learning program called Future Travelers, helping numerous megachurches become missional movements. Known for his innovative approach to mission, Alan is a teacher and key mission strategist for churches across the Western world. His popular book *The Shaping of Things to Come* (with Michael Frost) is widely considered to be a seminal text on mission. Alan's book *The Forgotten*

Ways has quickly become a key reference for missional thinking, particularly as it relates to missional movements. His book *ReJesus* (again with Frost) is a radical restatement about the role Jesus plays in defining Christian movements. *Untamed* (with his wife Debra) is about missional discipleship for a missional church. His most recent book, *Right Here, Right Now* (with Lance Ford), is about everyday mission for anyone.

Alan's experience in leadership includes leading a local church movement among the marginalized, developing training systems for innovative missional leadership, and heading up the Mission and Revitalization work of his denomination. He is series editor for the Shapevine Missional book series as well as an associate editor for *Leadership Journal*. Alan is an adjunct professor at Fuller Seminary, George Fox Seminary, and Wheaton, and lectures frequently throughout Australia, Europe, and the US.

From Missional Experts
ALAN HIRSCH & MICHAEL FROST

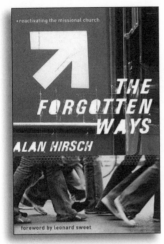

978-1-58743-164-7

978-1-58743-249-1

978-0-8010-4631-5

978-0-8010-4630-8

BrazosPress
a division of Baker Publishing Group
www.BrazosPress.com

BakerBooks
a division of Baker Publishing Group
www.BakerBooks.com

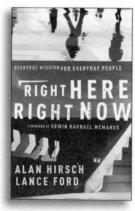
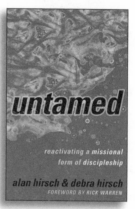
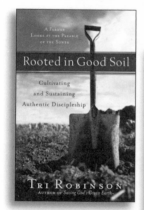

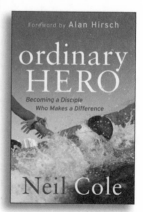

the forgotten ways

developing apostolic imagination and practice in Western contexts

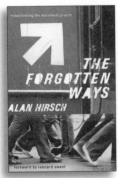

Visit **www.theforgottenways.org** to engage with Alan Hirsch on the ideas he presents in this book. You will also find significant resources that will help you implement some of the book's insights. One such resource is an online assessment of ministry related to the APEPT model as articulated by Alan in chapter 6 of *The Forgotten Ways*. This is a unique test that involves something of a 360-degree assessment on each applicant—an invaluable tool in trying to understand how God has shaped your ministry and leadership.

Another key tool is mPULSE. This unique online assessment measures the missional nature of your church or organization. It can be used as a stand-alone assessment; however, it is specifically designed to assist in applying concepts found in *The Forgotten Ways*, Alan's seminal book on missional movements based squarely on the Apostolic model. mPULSE provides an overview identifying the missional strengths and weaknesses of a church, church plant, missional movement, or organization. mPULSE also provides the respondents with a report and a suggested action plan to aid strategic planning and implementation. It is also designed to work with the very practical workbook *The Forgotten Ways Handbook*, as well as *On The Verge*. mPULSE can be used to assist as a diagnostic to aid in transition from traditional church growth models of ministry to the more organic missional ministry style.

www.theforgottenways.org